A PENNSYLVANIA QUAKER
IN
ANDERSONVILLE

THE DIARY OF
CHARLES SMEDLEY

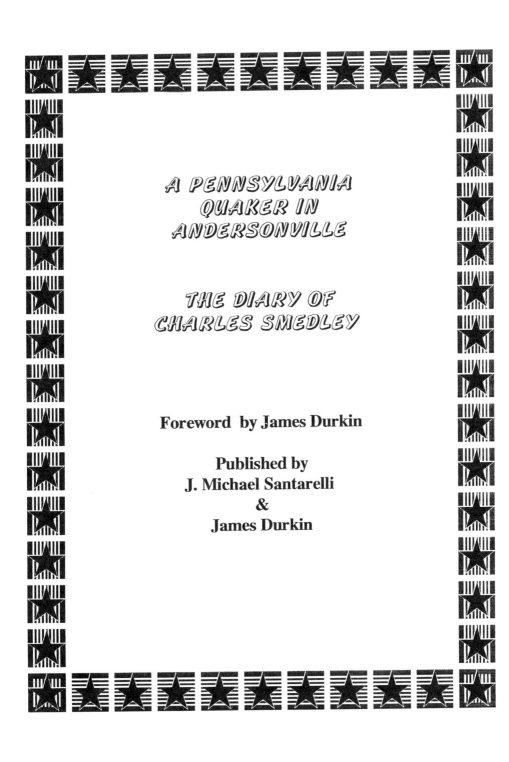

A PENNSYLVANIA QUAKER IN ANDERSONVILLE

THE DIARY OF CHARLES SMEDLEY

Foreword by James Durkin

Published by
J. Michael Santarelli
&
James Durkin

Originally published as Life in Southern Prisons

1865

Fulton, County Aid Society

Fulton Township, Lancaster County, Pennsylvania

International Standard Book Number 0-9631314-2-7

Please direct all correspondence and orders to:

J. Michael Santarelli Publishing
226 Paxson Ave.
Glenside, PA 19038

The Regimental Shield
The National Guards Regiment
The 90th Pennsylvania
Volunteer Infantry

The publishers wish to acknowledge the assistance of the
the following institutions:

Lancaster County Historical Society
Lancaster, Pennsylvania

The Civil War Library & Museum
Philadelphia, Pennsylania

The Grand Army of the Republic Museum
Philadelphia, Pennsylvania

Cover Artwork is Kim Gromoll's
conception of Charles Smedley shortly
after his arrival at Andersonville.

Foreword

It began, as all things do, with a single act. In November 1863 Confederate Secretary of War, James Seddon, ordered Captain Sidney Winder to consult with authorities in Georgia, then to select a site for a prison camp. Winder eventually chose a location five hundred yards east of the railroad depot at Anderson Station, not far from Americus, Georgia. When the project began there were no indications of the horror and death which would follow. In the days to come much would go wrong. Poor judgment and bad decisions contributed to the disaster which soon developed. The prison would become a death camp for a number of reasons: ignorance, stupidity, bad management, political necessity, and a measure of brutality and bitterness. All these things would become evident as events developed. For now, however, only the site had been selected and the future was still unknown.

At the end of December 1863, Captain Richard B. Winder proceeded to Andersonville(the name had been changed by the U.S. Postal Service in the 1850's to avoid confusion with Anderson, South Carolina) to begin construction of a stockade for the confinement of six thousand prisoners of war. Captain Winder had difficulties immediately. He found it necessary to impress the labor and tools needed to build the prison. Winder first had to get the authority for impressment from Richmond, slowing construction of the stockade. The authorities in Richmond began shipping prisoners to Andersonville on February 18, 1864. When the first prisoners arrived in Georgia on February 27th the stockade was unfinished. Captain Winder placed the prisoners under the muzzles of two guns loaded with canister. In this way he successfully maintained order until the work crews completed the stockade walls.

The stockade consisted of about sixteen acres of ground enclosed by a solid wall of twenty foot logs placed five feet into the ground. A small stream ran through the stockade yard dividing it almost in half. In finishing construction and making arrangements for the prisoner's needs, Captain Winder experienced shortages of every kind—lack of tools and wood for shelter, lack of food, lack of fuel to cook with, lack of water to drink, lack of soap and water for cleaning—all of which would have significant impact on the prisoner's survival. Additionally, the Captain made a serious error in placing the cookhouse, locating it upstream of the stockade, resulting in the waste from the building polluting the drinking water for the prisoners inside. Ovid L. Futch, in his History of Andersonville Prison, summed it up by saying:

"It is fairly obvious that part of the suffering and death at Andersonville was attributable to the paucity of developed southern resources. What may be less obvious, though no less important, is that some of it came as a result of short sighted management and lack of administrative ability."[1]

As a steady stream of prisoners began arriving at the prison, the authorities made a decision which had terrible consequences for the inmates of the stockade. The first prisoners, discovering that they were without shelter of any kind, soon constructed rude huts from whatever materials they could find. In permitting this, the Confederate authorities lost control of the interior of the prison. The random construction of shelter by the prisoners made proper policing of the interior of the stockade impossible. As the prison population increased in size, and more and more men were crowded into the stockade, sanitary conditions in Andersonville became totally unacceptable. Filth and human waste appeared throughout the camp. Since no effective policing program existed, disease and death ran unchecked throughout the prison population.

In April 1864 a group of prisoners arrived in Andersonville who had terrorized the prison camp at Belle Isle in Virginia. This was the same hard core group of Yankee prisoners who would become infamous as the "raiders." These men soon began to prey on their weak and helpless fellow prisoners. Led by William Collins of the

vii

88th Pennsylvania Volunteers, known as Moseby, the "raiders" soon engaged in a pattern of robbery and murder to obtain whatever they needed to survive. From April to the end of June these thugs continued their depredations unchecked. Finally, toward the end of June, the decent prisoners inside the stockade appealed to Captain Henry Wirz for assistance. Working together, the prisoners and the Confederate authorities, sought out and arrested the worst of the hoodlums. On June 30th General Winder issued General Order#57 authorizing the prisoners to establish a court to bring charges and impose punishment against the robbers and murderers among them. The six worst offenders—Pat Delaney, Charles Curtis, William Collins, John Sarsfield, Cary Sullivan, and A. Munn—were tried, convicted, and executed. On July 11th the prisoners imposed sentence on the six condemned men, hanging them inside the stockade, with the full blessing of the Confederate authorities. While this did not completely end predatory behavior inside the stockade, the problem of "raiding" never again became as prevalent as it had been before these executions.

Near the end of June the overcrowding in the stockade reached a critical point, the prison population reached more than 22,000 by the end of that month. The prison authorities responded to this problem by extending the size of the camp to twenty-six acres. The newly enlarged stockade walls now measured about 540 yards from east to west and about 260 yards on the shorter north to south walls. Unfortunately, the prison population expanded as well, to almost 32,000 by the end of July. The daily physical needs of these large numbers produced even worse conditions inside the stockade. The inadequacy of the sinks constructed along the banks of the stream led the prisoners to evacuate their bowels in the swamp. The resulting accumulation of filth from thousands of men, made the swamp a source of disease to the entire prison population. Maggots, mosquitoes, worms, and flies found an excellent breeding ground in this pile of filth, and disease was more easily spread as a result. Given the overcrowded conditions, lack of sanitation, demoralization of the prisoners(one soldier later wrote, "All you do is answer at roll–call; draw your rations, and fight lice."[2]), and the lack of nourishment the excessive death rate was inevitable. In the first three months of operation about 1,000 prisoners died in Andersonville. This occurred before the prison became overcrowded and was a result of disease which many prisoners brought with them from Belle Isle. Once the spring rains and the summer heat came; the prisoners, their clothing in rags, living amid piles of filth, exposed to insects and disease, died in increasing numbers.

By the time Andersonville went out of existence in April 1865, almost 13,000 Yankee soldiers were buried in mass graves outside the stockade. Northern newspapers lost no time in whipping public opinion to a frenzy. Once Brigadier General John H Winder, Confederate Commissary General of prisoners, died from a heart attack on February 6, 1865; the cry for revenge landed firmly on the head of Major Henry Wirz, who commanded the interior of the Andersonville stockade. Winder may have been the only man the prisoners hated more than Wirz, and with his death Wirz's position as scapegoat for the Andersonville deaths was secured. In what was the closest thing to a publicly sanctioned lynching in the history of the United States, Henry Wirz was tried and found guilty of crimes relating to the administration of the Andersonville prison camp.

A Military Court found Major Wirz guilty of the murder of ten prisoners inside the stockade. However, the identities of all ten victims were unknown to any other of the 32,000 prisoners confined in the camp. Major Wirz was also convicted of committing four murders during the month of August 1864, while he was on sick leave and not present at the prison camp. In addition, the court found Wirz guilty of conspiracy with other Confederate authorities to, "impair the health and destroy the lives of prisoners of war." Some of those who testified against Henry Wirz clearly perjured themselves. Wirz's ability to call witnesses for the defense was blatantly interfered with. The result was a foregone conclusion. The military court found the defendant guilty of both charges. The government executed Henry Wirz, hanging him on November 10, 1865 in Washington, D.C. The Andersonville Commandant was the only man on either side tried, convicted, and executed for "war crimes".

Charles Smedley joined the 90th Pennsylvania Volunteers on May 29, 1862. This young soldier did not have to serve. As a Quaker, he was a member of the New Britain Friends Meeting in Lancaster, Pennsylvania, Charles Smedley could have joined a Medical Unit and served as a conscientious objector. He chose instead to go into the army as a private soldier in a combat unit. In doing this Smedley risked being disowned by both his family and the Society of Friends. Private Smedley was fortunate. Neither his family nor the Friends disowned him.

The young Quaker proved to be a good soldier. The rebels captured him as the 90th Pennsylvania retreated from Chinn Ridge on August 30, 1862. Paroled in a few days by the Confederates, Private Smedley returned home to visit his family. He remained there until he was exchanged in early 1863. Charles rejoined the regiment in time to take part in the fighting at Chancellorsville and Gettysburg. In the Gettysburg fighting, he suffered two minor gunshot wounds, but remained in the line of battle. He was rewarded after Gettysburg with a promotion to Corporal. On the first day of the struggle in the Wilderness in May 1864, Charles Smedley was again captured. This captivity did not end as well as the first. The Confederate Government transported these prisoners to the deep south for better security. This had fatal consequences for Charles Smedley and thousands of prisoners like him.

When the 90th Pennsylvania Regiment mustered out in front of Petersburg in November 1864 Charles Smedley appeared on the rolls of Company G as, "Missing in action." The remarks beside his name on the final muster roll of Company G read, "An exemplary soldier." Based on his actions in both Andersonville and Florence, in caring for his friends and comrades, the entry could just as properly have read, "An exemplary human being."

The diary of Corporal Charles Smedley, Company G, 90th Pennsylvania Volunteers was published in 1865, by a committee of friends, only months after it was written. This publication was extremely limited. Only four hundred copies were issued when the diary was published in 1865, making it one of the rarest eyewitness accounts of Andersonville . The diary is very short. On some days Charles Smedley could manage to write only a single line. In spite of this, the soldier presents a good picture of the day to day struggle to survive in the Confederacy's worst prisoner of war camp. What makes the diary valuable today is that it was never embellished, as some others were, years after they were written. After his stay at Andersonville, Corporal Smedley moved on to the camp at Florence, South Carolina, when the Confederacy relocated thousands of Andersonville inmates to put them out of reach of General Sherman's advancing armies. After October 24, 1864 Charles Smedley could no longer write in his diary, due to sores on his hands. He suffered from chronic diarrhea throughout his imprisonment and died in the Florence camp on November 16, 1864.

What is most noticeable about the Smedley diary is the absence of atrocity stories. There are no murdering guards, no monstrous behavior by Major Wirz, and no accusations of any Confederate plot to commit mass murder. [Although the committee which published the diary believed differently.] Charles Smedley describes the day to day struggle for survival by himself and his friends. He frequently talks about the lack of food and water, the terrible filth, the demoralization of the prisoners, the lack of medical care, and the constant presence of death. There is, however, no accusation that the Confederate authorities engaged in any plot to kill their captives. In this regard the diary of Corporal Smedley is one of the most unbiased accounts produced by any Yankee prisoner of war held captive in the south's deadliest prison camp. Perhaps this accounts for its lack of widespread circulation on publication. By war's end, the north was whipped to a frenzy for revenge over the "atrocities" committed at Andersonville. Any document not describing such crimes was not likely to be given wide attention.

This diary is concerned mainly with Andersonville prison. It must be noted, however, that many other camps became death traps for the prisoners held within them. The prison camps operated by the United States Government were just as deadly as those in the Confederacy. The United States could not even claim the poor excuse of lack of resources as a reason for the high death rates. There is a story told by a Yankee prisoner about another prisoner in Andersonville who assessed the blame for his condition as follows:

"I remember having my attention called one day by the most terrible oaths coming from a man on the side hill, just out of the swamp. I went close to him. He seemed to be delirious. He lay there with maggots and worms crawling in and out of his ears and nose; lice all over him; flies buzzing around; maggots and worms between his fingers and toes. And there he lay, seemingly without strength to move, and from his mouth there poured the most fearful string of oaths I ever heard. It seemed he blamed President Lincoln for not arranging an exchange, and on his head fell the burden of the oaths. He also cursed the Union, cursed the Confederacy, and cursed God for permitting his condition. He lay in that condition, cursing and moaning, for several days before he died."[3]

Certainly, when blame is assessed for the horrors of prisoner of war camps, both north and south, there is blame enough and shame enough for both sides to share.

James Durkin
March 1995

1.   History of Andersonville Prison, Ovid L. Futch, University of Florida Press, 1968, Page 12.

2.   The Smoked Yank, Melvin Grigsby, 2nd Edition, The Regan Printing Co., Chicago, 1891, Page 98.

3.   Ibid., Page 135.

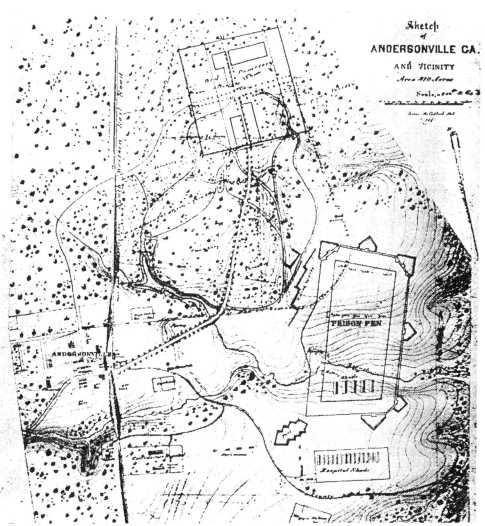

A postwar sketch of the area of Andersonville, Georgia which
includes the prison compound.

A PENNSYLVANIA QUAKER IN ANDERSONVILLE

THE DIARY OF CHARLES SMEDLEY

The Second Review of The Grand Armies

By Bret Harte

I read last night of the grand review
In Washington's chiefest avenue—
Two hundred thousand men in blue
I think they said was the number—
Till I seemed to hear their tramping feet,
The bugle's blast, and the drum's quick beat,
The clatter of hoofs in the stony street,
The cheers of the people who came to greet,
And the thousand details that to repeat
Would only my verse encumber—
Till I in a revery sad and sweet,
And then to a fitful slumber.

When, Lo! in a vision I seemed to stand,
In a lonely Capitol. On each hand
Far stretched the portico, dim and grand,
Its columns ranged like a martial band
Of sheeted specters, whom some command
Had called to the last reviewing!
And the streets of the City were white
and bare,
No footfalls echoed along the square,
But out of the musty midnight air
I heard in the distance a trumpet blare,
And the wandering night winds seemed to bear
The sound of a far tattooing.

Then I held my breath in fear and dread,
For into the square with a brazen tread,
There rode a figure whose stately head
O'erlooked the review that morning.
It never bowed from its firm set seat
When the living column passed its feet,
Yet now rode stately up the street
To the phantom's bugle warning,
Till it reached the Capitol Square and
wheeled,
And there in the moonlight stood revealed
A well known form, that in state and field
Had led our patriot sires;
Whose face was turned to the sleeping camp,
Afar through the river's fog and damp,
That showed no flicker nor waning lamp,
Nor wasted bivouac fires.

And I saw a phantom army come,
With never a sound of fife or drum,
But keeping time to a throbbing hum
Of wailing and lamentation!
The martyred heroes of Malvern Hill,
Of Gettysburg and Chancellorsville.
The men whose wasted figures fill
The patriot graves of the Nation.
And there come the nameless dead, the
men
Who perished in fever swamp and fen,
The slowly starved of the prison pen!
And, marching beside the others,
Come the dusky martyrs of Pillow's
fight,
With limbs enfranchised and bearing
bright;
I thought—perhaps 'twas the pale
moonlight—
They looked as white as their brothers.

And so all night marched the Nation's
dead,
With never a banner above them spread,
Nor a badge nor a motto brandished!
No mark—save the bare uncovered head
of the silent bronze reviewer—
With never an arch but the vaulted sky,
With never a flower save those that lie
On the distant graves—for love could
buy
No gift that was purer or truer.

So all night long swept the strange
array,
So all night long till the morning
gray
I watched for one who had passed
away,
With a reverent awe and wonder,
Till a blue cap waved in the
lengthening line,
And I knew that one who was kin of
mine,
Had come, and I spoke—and Lo!
that sign
Awakened me from my slumber.

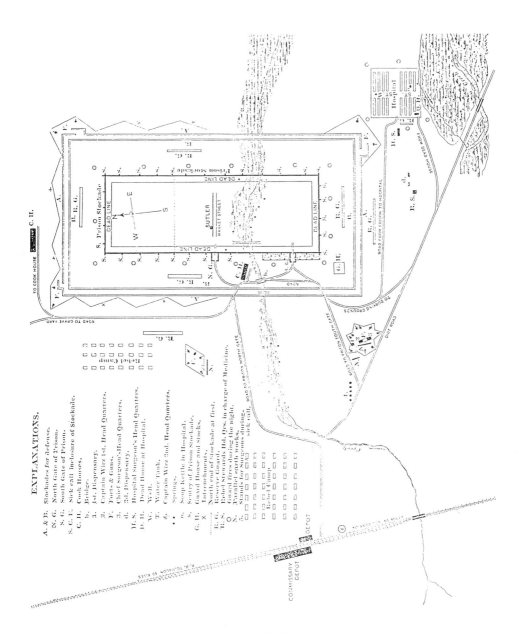

The Andersonville Prison Compound

April 7, 1865. At a regular meeting of the FULTON AID SOCIETY "New Business" being in order, the following resolutions were offered and unanimously adopted:

Resolved, That the "Fulton Aid Society" request of the friends of the late Charles Smedley, that a copy of his diary, kept while a prisoner at Andersonville, Georgia, be furnished for the purpose of publication.

Resolved, That a Committee consisting of four members of the association be appointed to receive the manuscript, prepare it for publication, and that it be authorized to have printed an edition of four hundred copies for the use of the Society.

In conformity with the above resolutions, the following were appointed the committee:

> CHAS. H. STUBBS, M.D., Chairman.
> JAMES H. CLARK
> ANNIE SMEDLEY
> ELWOOD SMEDLEY

Map of
Fulton Township,
Lancaster County,
Pennsylvania

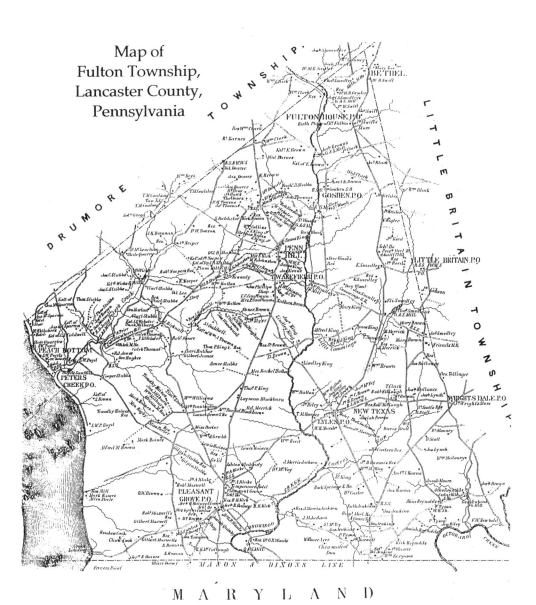

P R E F A C E

The following pages contain a plain, unvarnished statement of facts that occurred under the notice of one who was so unfortunate as to be taken prisoner by those who sought to destroy and dissever our glorious country. As will be perceived, it is written with great care, hence its reliability.

It was thought best to print the author's diary, just as it was received, without any amplification, save that absolutely necessary for the press. To the reader we will say that Dr. Buckley was one of our surgeons who fell into the hands of the Confederates. Corporal William Griffith, of Company G, 90th Regiment P.V., was taken prisoner along with Charles Smedley. He is spoken of as "Griffith."

With these few explanations we offer this little book to our citizens, feeling confident that it will be purchased and read by many of them.

In purchasing this work you contribute your mite towards alleviating the condition of those whose sufferings are so well set forth in its pages.

COMMITTEE ON PUBLICATION.

A Biographical Sketch

of Charles Smedley

By Chas. H. Stubbs, M.D.

CHARLES SMEDLEY, eldest son of Joel and Martha Smedley,was born in Fulton Township, Lancaster County, Pennsylvania, on the first day of November, 1836. Until his nineteenth year he remained at home, assisting his father in farming during the Summer seasons, and in the Winter attending the public school of the district. Having mastered the elementary branches usually taught in the district schools, and desiring to acquire a knowledge of higher scientific studies, he entered as a student in the celebrated Friends' School at Westtown, on the seventh of May, 1855. While at this institution, he pursued the studies he had chosen with great diligence and success. By close application he attained an honorable standing in his class; and his strict deportment merited the high approbation of his preceptors and the confidence of all his companions.

On the eleventh of April, 1856, after spending nearly a year at Westtown, he returned home and again assisted his father in superintending the mills and managing the farm. This engaged his attention for the next two years.

In the Spring of 1858 he concluded to commence business for himself. That of a merchant suggested itself; but feeling deficient in knowledge necessary to success if he engaged in this business, he resolved to prepare himself by taking a mercantile course. With this object in view, on the fifth of May, 1858, he

7

entered the Lancaster County Normal School at Millersville. While at Millersville he became an active and influential member of the Page Society—a noted literary association connected with the Normal School.

Having remained one term at the Normal School, he returned to his native place in the Fall, and on the thirteenth of October, 1858, entered into an agreement with his father to take the grist and the saw mills "on the shares." He continued to have charge of the two mills for two years, and met with good success. During these two years he took an active interest in every movement that would have a tendency to improve the moral condition of society.

Believing strongly in the influence to be exerted by example, he joined several associations, whose object was of a reformatory character. Uniting himself with the Odd Fellows and Good Templars, he took an active part in the business of both of these orders. In these associations he was among the first to see that the rules were implicitly obeyed and kept inviolate. On one occasion a fellow member of the order of Odd Fellows was on trial for violating one of the sworn conditions on which he entered the lodge, by persisting in getting intoxicated whenever he felt disposed. The member who was most opposed to continuing this habitual drunkard in the lodge was Charles Smedley. In his little speech made in opposition, he boldly and fearlessly asserted that it was immaterial what position the person on trial might occupy— by his late actions the accused had unfitted himself to be continued any longer in the association, and in his opinion should be expelled.

In the Order of Good Templars Charles Smedley attained the highest position of the lodge of which he was a member. Through his influence many other young men were induced to join and forever eschew that accursed evil which has led to the ruin of many noble youths and caused them to fill premature graves.

On the twenty–first of April 1862, he gave up his interest in the mills, having in contemplation a visit to some of the northern

8

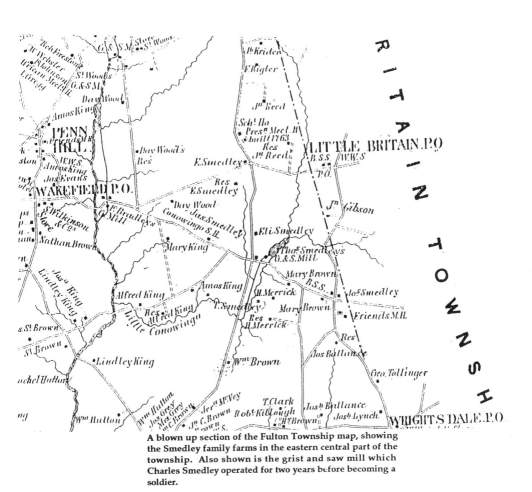

A blown up section of the Fulton Township map, showing the Smedley family farms in the eastern central part of the township. Also shown is the grist and saw mill which Charles Smedley operated for two years before becoming a soldier.

cities. After traveling several weeks in central New York, and spending a few days in the great Eastern Metropolis, young Smedley returned to Pennsylvania on the twenty-first of May.

The great rebellion had now been in progress for a year. Throughout the sections of the country visited by him, the young men of the North were rapidly volunteering for their country's defense. Thinking it was not right for him to travel now and spend his time, he came home with the determination of serving his country in her hour of peril.

Well knowing that the consent of his parents could not be obtained,(they being members of the Society of Friends, one of the most important tenets of which is a "testimony against war,")he bid them adieu and started for Philadelphia, where, on the 29th of May, 1862, he enlisted as a member of Company G, 90th Regiment Pennsylvania Volunteers.

For some the life of a soldier has its attractions. The sound of martial music, the gay uniform, the novelty of camp life, and the desire for fame—all contribute to allure many into the military service. None of these inducements had any weight with Charles Smedley. No one had a greater hatred of war; but like many others, he felt that this war was prosecuted on the part of the North for *National existence,* and as such differed from wars of aggression. Hence he thought it was *his duty,* as it was the duty of every man, to assist in putting down the rebellion. Maintaining these views, and from motives of the highest patriotism, Charles Smedley joined the army "for three years or the war."

In a letter written to the author of this sketch, soon after he enlisted, dated Front Royal, 6th mo. 16th, 1862," he says: "After traveling through the different parts of the country and witnessing the state of things caused by this rebellion, I by degrees made up my mind that the larger the force that we could put in the field the sooner would this rebellion be crushed, and it was the duty of every person, who could, to volunteer. Having no business to require my attention, that I liked, and believing that if ever I lent my aid in suppressing this rebellion, now was the time, hence my present situation."

In a letter dated "6th mo. 19th, 1862," addressed to one of his relatives, in answer to the question, "how he liked soldiering?" he replied: "If I were at home, perhaps I would find more pleasure; but to take everything into consideration, it is every man's duty to try and put down this rebellion. I did not expect to like a soldier's life when I left home, but can honestly say that I like it better than I expected to."

From a letter written to his parents, dated, "7th mo. 4th, 1862," we take the following beautiful and patriotic sentiments: "I am sorry to hear that you cannot help being uneasy about me. This regiment, as yet, has not been in any dangerous positions, ad may not during the war. As far as myself is concerned, I have no fears and feel it my duty to go wherever the regiment is ordered. The question often comes into my mind, 'Have I done right?' To this my conscience answers that I have, and must continue to do my duty. The longer I remain the more firmly I am impressed that I am doing nothing but my simple duty and all will come out right in the end. And being thus impressed I move along with a light heart and nothing to fear. To be frank, I put my trust in the Almighty ruler above, and believe whatever *my fate shall be*, will be in accordance with His will. I know that my course is very inconsistent with our discipline,* but I believe that at present I owe a higher duty to my country. I hope that it may be restored to us, more peaceful and prosperous than ever; and if it is my fortune to get back safely home, I can congratulate myself upon having done my duty."

From Philadelphia, after enlisting, Charles Smedley was sent to Washington, and from thence to Front Royal, a small town west of the Blue Ridge, where the 90th Regiment was then encamped. He joined it just previous to the advance of our forces sent to intercept "Stonewall" Jackson, in his progress down the Shenandoah Valley. He continued with the regiment, and was with it up to the time of the second Battle of Bull Run. For more than a week previous to this engagement, he had made application to be sent to

*Reference is here made to the Friend's discipline--he being a member by birthright

11

the hospital, being weak and exhausted from disease. On the morning of the battle, he declared he would not send in his application to be sent to the rear, because the impression might exist that he was trying to evade duty in time of danger. By almost superhuman exertion he managed to go into the fight, but in the retreat of our forces, becoming fatigued and prostrated, he was compelled to remain in the rear, and the consequence was he fell into the hands of the enemy.

In a few days he was paroled and forwarded to our lines, and then sent by the Federal authorities to Annapolis, Maryland. He arrived home on the 29th of October, 1862, and remained until the 18th of February, 1863, when he was regularly exchanged.

Joining the regiment a second time, he continued with it over thirteen months. While in the service he participated in the Battles of Cedar Mountain, Second Bull Run, Rappahannock Station, Chancellorsville, Thoroughfare Gap, Gettysburg, and the Wilderness. In all these battles young Smedley performed his duty nobly. In the first day's fight at Gettysburg he narrowly escaped with his life—a ball grazing him on the neck and another on the hip. In the second and third day's fights the 90th Regiment was engaged on the memorable Cemetery ridge. After the defeat of the rebel hordes on the heights of Gettysburg, our army followed the remainder of the enemy's forces to the banks of the Rapidan. While encamped on this stream, the subject of our sketch received the sad news of affliction among "the loved ones at home." His mother, brother, and sister being dangerously ill—the two former dying soon afterwards.

From a letter written to his sister on the reception of the sad intelligence, we copy the following: "It is a great trial to me to have to be separated from you when I think of the present state of things. Perhaps all is for the best, and we should not complain. We are but poor creatures and must submit to the Almighty ruler who holds our fate in the 'hollow of his hand.' In the language of the christian, 'Why should we not put our trust in Him, and pray for Him to bring us out of all our trials and afflictions?' Perhaps we

have not been thankful enough for all the blessings we enjoy. Give
my love to all my old friends. I often think of the many pleasant
times we have had at home. I hope I may again have the pleasure of
meeting you all there, and not say, as Byron, of home,

> 'Fare thee well, and if forever,
> Still, forever fare thee well.'"

—

At the Battle of the Wilderness, on the 5th of May, 1864,
Charles Smedley was captured a second time, and as we are informed
in his diary, was taken by the Confederates to Gordonsville, thence
to Danville, from Danville to the prisoners' pen at Andersonville,
Georgia, and lastly to Florence, South Carolina. At Andersonville
he remained nearly four months in a stockade filled with thousands
of Northern patriots. Here he suffered untold hardships, being
exposed to the scorching rays of the sun, the cold atmosphere of
the night, and to the frequent storms of rain. The premeditated,
gradual starvation process of his vile captors, together with the
constant exposure to all kinds of weather, did its work
effectually. His health at last became impaired and his physical
constitution forever shattered. On the thirteenth of September,
along with many others, he reached the town of Florence, where he
was placed in another pen, in every respect similar to the one he
had left at Andersonville. Here his sufferings increased. Being
much reduced, and possessing hardly sufficient strength to assist
himself, he was at last admitted into what was termed a hospital.
In this hospital he lingered along for a few weeks, when his system
gradually succumbed from the effects of hunger and exposure.

During the night of the sixteenth of November, 1864, the spirit
of Charles Smedley left its mortal tenement for other realms. His
body was prepared for burial by a few of his fellow soldiers, and
was interred in the burying ground a short distance north—northwest
of the stockade, in Florence, South Carolina.

In the person of Charles Smedley there were nicely blended many
of the noblest traits of human character. As a religious and moral
young man he had few equals. From his early youth he had a strong
aversion to all those evil habits which have so often been the

stepping stones to vice in its most hideous forms. Profanity and the use of that filthy narcotic weed, proved harmless as tempters to him. Still less powerful was that subtle enemy of mankind, which "quickeneth and giveth color to the cup, and stingeth like an adder."*

In all his transactions his rule was to do that only which his conscience told him was right. His goodness of heart, his amiable disposition, gained him many friends, and wherever known, whether at home in his native township, or in the army of his country, none knew him other than the noble young man and soldier.

Today the remains of Charles Smedley, along with those of thousands of other patriotic martyrs, lie in the trenches near Florence. No marble pile or grass covered mound will, in all probability, ever mark his last resting place, but his name will ever be cherished and held in remembrance by his friends, as one who was willing to offer up his life that his country might live.

*In a letter to his father, dated 8th mo. 16th, 1863, written while the army was at Rappahannock Station, we find the following extract: "When I enlisted, I made a resolution that I, as long as I was in the service, would neither use profane language, smoke or chew tobacco, or drink intoxicating liquors. This resolution I have strictly adhered to, and I believe I am a happier man for it."

A sketch shows the civilian Charles Smedley before he joined the
National Guards Regiment in 1862.

Diary
From the Wilderness
to
Florence Prison Pen

1st day, 5th mo.1st, 1864.   Camp near Mitchell's Station, Va. Had regimental inspection this morning at ten o'clock by Captain William Davis.   The parade was formed, then moved to the rear into columns, and as we were critically inspected yesterday, we were dismissed.   I was busy the rest of the day helping Johnson to fix up the clothing books, and as the pay rolls were not right, we had to go to work and make out three more, leaving out ten deserters, which were taken up wrong on them at first.   J.C. Kimball wrote one while Johnson and I wrote the others.   Received my Baltimore American.

2nd day, 5th mo. 2nd.   Done nothing of any account all day.   Was nice weather.

3rd day, 5th mo. 3rd.   This was a nice warm day.   Each company was out at target practice one or two hours this afternoon.   Each of us shot five rounds.   Some talk of us moving.

4th day, 5th mo. 4th.   We were told at nine last evening to have everything packed, as we would likely have to move.   Drew six days rations of coffee, sugar, and crackers, two days rations of pork. We were called up at twelve o'clock last night, packed up, and by three o'clock were on the march.   Marched towards Piney Mountain, where we arrived about sunrise, and made a short halt. We were in the rear of the First Brigade.   Marched past Stephensburg, thence crossed the Rapidan at twelve o'clock on a pontoon bridge.   There were two bridges of canvas covered boats at Germania Ford. After stopping a short time, took up the march and followed the Plank Road, and after going five or eight miles, halted and bivouacked for the night on a high hill near the right of the road.   The day was very warm after the sun rose. We were forced as fast as it was possible for us to go—stragglers fell out by hundreds—no brigade or regiment seemed to be together in the after part of the day. I had to fall out, and threw away my mess kettle, some of my clothes, pork, and several other things, and then could no more than keep up. Halted with the little part of the regiment, took a good bath, and made supper of bread, pork, and coffee. We seemed to be in the rear and with the General's headquarters. Went to bed on the ground about 8 P.M.

5th day, 5th mo. 5th. Five o'clock A.M. Slept well last night. Were called up at three this morning, got our breakfasts and made ready to move. Are now awaiting orders. The birds are playing around us and the day promises to be a pleasant one. Seven A.M. Have moved out and halted to the right of the road—are six miles from Mine Run and fifteen from Fredericksburg. General Warren's headquarters are near us. We appear to be pretty well in the rear. Colonel _____ commands the First Brigade. Have not heard of any rebels yet in front. General Burnside is said to be in the rear guarding fifteen hundred wagons. The sun is coming out hot—the weather clear and sultry. Twelve M. [Noon] Have been lying down since six o'clock. The Sixth Corps has passed down the Plank Road to take position on our left. Heard some heavy musketry firing towards our left. It is said to be all calvary fighting. From what I know we are in the reserve. General Robinson's headquarters are within a hundred yards of us. There is also a signal station near the headquarters. This is near the Wilderness Tavern. There is a house on the hill where "Stonewall" Jackson was taken after he was wounded at Chancellorsville. The sun is burning hot.

6th day, 5th mo. 6th. Nine o'clock A.M. At one o'clock yesterday we advanced as a forward guard center, we being the third regiment in line from the position we occupied at 12 M. Kept on through the woods for half a mile, then the other regiment halted and deployed, and helped us on the second line, with our right resting on the turnpike. The front line was busily engaged as we advanced—the bullets flew thick and fast around us, mostly high.

17

About two o'clock we advanced the second time, about two hundred yards, and lay down under a heavy fire where we remained until six o'clock. All the time we lay under a fire from the rebels, who were less than a quarter of a mile off. They had a battery on the left of the pike which occasionally threw shells and solid shot in good range over us, cutting off the limbs of trees; only a few were low enough to come near us. One solid shot lit in the centre of our company, and plowed the ground up under Audenried's feet, [Private Adam Audenreid, a substitute, was later captured at Weldon Railroad on August 19, 1864.] bursting his canteen and throwing the dirt over the men around him, without doing any more damage. At six o'clock P.M., an officer, I do not know who, [General Griffin who was a division commander, V Army Corps.] came up and gave us the order to, "Advance with the 39th Massachusetts." After the order was repeated twice, we started, going over dead and wounded who had been slaughtered by hundreds, and lay thick on the ground we went over. The rebels did not fire a shot until we got out into the open plain, and then they opened with grape and canister and volleys of musketry. After going to the bottom of the hill and up halfway toward the enemy's battery, the Colonel gave the order to, "About face." I had stopped to cap my piece, and before I got it done the regiment was going back on double-quick. I followed in the rear, and coming to a ditch, fell into it, and on looking up saw our fellows going up the hill toward our line. The bullets flew so thick that I thought it the next thing to getting shot to get out of the ditch, and after a few moments concluded I had better stay where I was until after dark, and then get up the hill into our lines. I soon noticed that the ditch was full of men. After halloing to those above and below me, I found that Griffin, Edwards and Fry of our Company, [Private John Edwards, Private John Fry, and, probably, Private William Griffith, all of Company G; Fry and Griffith both died in Confederate prisons.] and one of Company B's men were near us. We all thought we had better stay where we were until after dark. I went to Edwards and there found a man who told us to lay still and he would take us off after a

18

while. Edwards asked him who he was. He said he was a Confederate officer. On looking up the ditch, which was deep above us, I saw some of the enemy's sharpshooters and skirmishers, and it was plain to be seen that we were in their power. The officer ordered us to disarm ourselves and it would be all right. We were taken, about half past seven o'clock, into the Confederate lines to the pike, then to the rear for about half a mile and kept under guard. As we were going off I found Sergeant M. of our company—picked him up and took him with us. He had been knocked down but was not hurt. Sergeant Riley I also picked up. [Cannot be further identified.] I told him how we were situated. Griffith gave him a canteen of water, and then we were ordered to come on. He was trying to play it, I thought. I am certain half our regiment was lost. Griffith and I went to work and made some coffee in a pot that I picked up in the morning. About nine P.M., twelve of our company and some more of the 90th were brought in. Everything, while I was awake, was quiet. Griffith and I made a bed and slept together. I did not get to sleep until after twelve o'clock. At day-break this morning I was awakened by artillery firing. I got up and went to the creek, got a pot of water and made some coffee, and then awakened Griffith and we took our breakfast. At six A.M. we were ordered to fall in; we got our things, and were marched to Robertson's Tavern, where we are at present. From seven to half past eight there was some very sharp musketry up the pike. The guards are busy trading with the boys; there are about fifty of us here. Ten A.M. All seems to be quiet in front. Night—Lay under guard all day; heard no fighting of any account today. Things appear to be quiet in front. The ambulances brought in a great many wounded men all day.

7th day, 5th mo. 7th. Were marched, some two hundred and seventy of us, to Orange Court House, then put aboard cars and taken to Gordonsville.

1st day, 5th mo. 8th. Kept here all day. Where we were last night we drew one day's rations of corn meal, beef, and salt. I was commissary for a squad of twenty-five men. Sent a letter home. The sun was burning hot.

2nd day, 5th mo. 9th. We were put into a house forty by fifty feet square last night and came near smothering. We were taken out this morning. Made mush for breakfast. Had to stay out in the sun all day. Part of us were sent to Lynchburg yesterday—some more came last night. Griffith and I laid down after supper to rest for the night. Drew one ration of corn meal and herring—three of the latter to each man.

3rd day, 5th mo. 10th. Soon after we got to bed last night we were ordered to pack up. Left Gordonsville in a train of cars at eleven o'clock at night, and after a hard night's travel got to this place (Lynchburg) about ten this morning. Were put in a deep ravine with a stream of water running through it. A heavy guard of citizens, consisting of old men, "played out" soldiers, and boys were around us. Two pieces of artillery are planted in range of us. I was with the first one hundred of our squad that came in today. We were put in charge of a Sergeant-Major, who drew rations for us. There was about one thousand came here yesterday. I got seven "hard tack" and some bacon for one day's rations. There are about 2,500 of us here. Today was burning hot.

4th day, 5th mo. 11th. Had a good sleep last night. This was a very warm day. There were seventy-five loaves of soft rye bread, half a peck of rice, and a little salt issued to a squad today. There were one thousand men sent away today.

5th day, 5th mo. 12th. It commenced to rain about nine o'clock last night. Griffith and I had a rough night of it—had to sit up a good part of the time, 'till the after part of the night, when we laid down under the woolen blanket. About daylight it commenced to rain rapidly. The water ran on us and caused us to get up and sit with the gum blanket over our shoulders. It rained pretty much all day; we had to sit most of the time with the gum blanket over us. With hard work we made some coffee for breakfast and some mush for

20

supper. Carried some flat stones to lay on tonight. Drew seventy-five loaves of bread for the balance of yesterday's rations; also for today, six "hard tack," pork and rice, to a man, for two days' rations.

6th day, 5th mo. 13th. Had a rough night of it. Slept under our woolen blankets until daylight. It rained a great deal all night—got considerably wet. Showery all day. About ten o'clock A.M. we were moved out of the ravine to the cars and got aboard at twelve, and were off for Danville. We were stowed as closely as possible in burden cars. Passed through Danville before dark. There are rebels hospitals at this place.

7th day, 5th mo. 14th. Traveling all night and until ten o'clock this forenoon, when we arrived at Danville. Here we were put into large houses. The house I am in is one hundred by forty-seven feet, three stories high. The two upper stories are only occupied by us, some five hundred in number. Here we were divided into messes of twenty each, and drawing two square inches of boiled bacon and a loaf of corn bread for two men.

1st day, 5th mo. 15th. Had a roll call at nine A.M. and were counted. Drew corn bread at ten o'clock and rice soup at four P.M., and soon after, boiled bacon. Got a pint of soup to a man. Can do nothing but lay down, or walk, or stand, after going to wash. There are five hundred in this building. We hear no news.

2nd day, 5th mo. 16th. Spent the day as yesterday. Drew some of our hard bread, Confederate bacon, and rice soup. There was a fellow selling toilet soap at the rate of one dollar and fifty cents Confederate script, or two cakes for a dollar greenback.

3rd day, 5th mo. 17th. Lay about all day. In the morning darned the toe of one of my stockings and mended my pantaloons, Sent a letter home to father. We are to be sent to Georgia tomorrow. Drew a day's rations for today of corn bread and boiled bacon for tomorrow.

21

4th day, 5th mo. 18th. Got up at daybreak, left the prison at six, got on the cars at half past eight and started at nine. At twelve came as far as the railroad was finished,(the Danville & Greensborough Railroad) then had to march six miles to where it commenced again, and then lay for an hour for three trains to come. After they arrived it took until long after dark to load them. I was among the last to get aboard.

5th day, 5th mo. 19th. Had a bad time of it last night—could not sit or stand with comfort. The rain came through the car so bad that I had to get out my "gum." We had only thirteen miles to go, and it was near daylight before we got to Greensborough, which was about six in the morning. Here we stopped about two hours, then went on, bound for Charlotte, North Carolina, where we arrived at half past six. The train went very slow all night, but after we left Greensborough, very fast. The country along the road was very, very poor. The only places of much note were High Point Station, Thomasville, and Lexington. Greensborough is a manufacturing town, but like in all other towns and villages, business was at a stand still. Thomasville was the prettiest place. There is a seminary there. Some ladies came out to the train and threw two ginger cakes at us, also some bouquets. Crossed the Yadkin River. After we got to Charlotte, were taken off the cars and marched to the railroad crossing. Drew rations of crackers and pork; I got six crackers and a chunk of pork for two days. A thunder gust came up which continued until ten o;clock. Griffith and I made out to kindle a little fire and make a pot of coffee. I was taken with a chill and fever of a bilious nature—can eat no supper. By eleven o'clock it cleared up and the moon shone out. Made our bed on the ground and were soon asleep.

6th day, 5th mo. 20th. Slept well last night, and got up at six o'clock A.M.; felt very bad and very bilious; got some hot water to make coffee, but could not find the coffee. The sun came out bright and hot this morning. At twelve M. were put aboard the cars. The cars moved past the town, backed, and moved forward and back, etc., until about six o'clock, when we were backed to the

22

southeast end of town. Each car load was taken off in separate squads of nineteen or twenty—drew rations for one day, three "hard tack" and a chunk of pork. I was sick all day with the chills and fever—no appetite; ate some souse, well peppered, but had to force it down. The day was very hot.

7th day, 5th mo. 21st. Slept well last night on the ground. The moon was full and the sky clear. We were ordered to pack up about six o'clock, and get on the same cars we got off. Griffith and I were so lucky as to get our old places in the stock cars; rode all day, and arrived at Columbia, South Carolina at sunset. After stopping there over an hour, we changed cars. We got larger cars but less of them. They crowded seventy-five men inside and on top, which nearly smothered us. The guard had orders not to let a man out, and to shoot the first person that attempted it. Our car is a close burden car, which was closed all around except one door. I was so lucky as to get near the door and have plenty of fresh air. By doubling up, made out to lie down, with my head next the door. This was a warm day, but we being in such a good car, rode comfortably. The country for two days' journey was poorer than any yet passed. Did not see much of Columbia. I felt very well all day; my disease is better. Took two doses of "composition" in cold water.

1st day, 5th mo. 22nd. I made out with difficulty to lay on my back last night. The guard, "the first half," sat on my head, and then laid down with head on my breast for a pillow—could not sleep. My feet and legs were doubled up, and I was lying on them part of the time, while others piled theirs on top of mine. This morning got a good seat by the door; rode there until we stopped at Augusta. Changed cars at this place at 12 o'clock M. Did not pass any place of importance after Charlotte. Stopped at dusk and had a loaf of bread and a chunk of pork issued to us. I had been rather bad with the diarrhea—was very weak and dizzy, with no appetite; but after drawing rations, felt like eating, and ate a bit of bread and pork; the bread is rye. When we changed cars I got a seat in the middle of the door. My door was shut at dark, so I had to set with my back against it.

2nd day, 5th mo. 23rd. Did not sleep much in the night, had to sit all the time. There were sixty–five men inside the box and some on top. At daylight the door was opened. I then rode with my legs out. Get to Marion about the middle of the day. Three trains were made of two, and we went at the rate of twenty–five miles an hour. Arrived at Andersonville, Georgia at five o'clock P.M., when we were taken off the cars, and counted off into squads with a sergeant, who took our names on a piece of paper which a rebel officer gave him. Then we were ordered into a large stockade and halted in the southeast corner of it. There we had the ground for our quarters. We concluded that it was hard to move about. Made our bed on the ground. Weather clear and hot. Yesterday passed Wanesville. Today passed Fort Valley after leaving Marion.

3rd day, 5th mo. 24th. Slept very well on the ground last night; arose at daylight, went to the run and took a good wash. Had roll–call and were counted by a rebel sergeant whose name is Warmer. There were ninety men in our mess. Drew rations at five o'clock P.M. Half a loaf of corn bread and half a square inch of bacon to each man. The bacon is excellent. There were three or four hundred more men put in here today. The place was much too crowded before. They brought them in on the main street and told them to go and find places wherever they *could*. Griffith and I having but fifteen cents in money, and that being mine, we are bad off. Bought two split pieces of pine, six feet long and two and a half inches square, to put up a shelter. These I purchased for my fifteen cents. These not being enough, I traded my looking glass for two more. Put up my woolen blanket over our ridge pole and now have a good place to stay in. This place contains about fifteen or twenty acres of ground, enclosed with a stockade twenty feet high, with a sentry stand every one hundred and fifty feet. There is a stream of water running through it with a hill extending up from each side of it. For thirty or more yards from the run the ground is swampy and has a bad smell coming from it.

24

4th day, 5th mo. 25th. Spent this day about the same as yesterday, laying in our tent, etc., etc. Drew the same kind of rations. More prisoners put in today.

5th day, 5th mo. 26th. This was a very hot day. There are men here just like skeletons, they are so far gone with the chronic diarrhea. The boys caught some of the raiders and punished them by shaving their heads. There are plenty of "sweat" boards in operation, and other kinds of gaming. Drew a loaf of corn bread, two thirds of a pint of mush, and four square inches of bacon for two of us. The cornmeal is of the roughest description not being *sifted.* Went to the run this morning and washed a pair of drawers and a shirt, and then took a bath myself.

6th day, 5th mo. 27th. Spent this day like yesterday, doing nothing. Drew a loaf of corn bread, three bits of meat, and nearly a pint of boiled rice. The pork today was all boiled jowls. The sun was scorching hot. Sent a few lines home to father.

7th day, 5th mo. 28th. Was a very warm day. One hundred and eighty more prisoners were put in here today from Sherman's army, making in all sixteen thousand six hundred and fifty(16,650). There are sixty—one detachments of two hundred and seventy each, not including what came today. Drew the usual quantity of corn bread, bacon, and mush to a man.

1st day, 5th mo. 29th. Was extremely warm. Lay in the "House" most of the time. There were about fifteen hundred more men put in here today. Did not draw rations until sundown, when we got pork and corn bread.

2nd day, 5th mo. 30th. This day was very oppressive. More prisoners came in today.

3rd day, 5th mo. 31st. Weather as hot as ever. Was at the stockade where the rebels throw over their produce. Greenbacks are worth twice as much as "scrip." Peas, beans, tobacco, onions, turnips, egg, cakes, groundnuts, etc., etc., are passed over in large quantities and sold at enormous prices. My disease seems worse and I am getting weak.

25

4th day, 6th mo. 1st. Was cloudy until the middle of the day, then had a heavy thunderstorm, and a little rain now and then until evening. I lay in the house most of the day—was very weak. We made some burnt corn bread crust coffee this morning. There were about four hundred more prisoners put in here today; none of them from the Potomac Army.

5th day, 6th mo. 2nd. This was the same kind of a day as yesterday, with more rain. Borrowed the Banner of Light from Dr. Buckley this afternoon.

6th day, 6th mo. 3rd. Was cloudy towards sundown, when there came up a heavy wind, followed by rain. The day was very warm. More prisoners put in today, mostly sick and wounded, captured when we were. The place is getting crowded full. Diarrhea no better

7th day, 6th mo. 4th. Had a good deal of rain. I lay in the house. Two hundred more came in today. There were a great many rumors about us being paroled or exchanged on the sixth. We split up the last of our wood with a musket screw–driver, and traded some corn bread for another stick.

1st day, 6th mo. 5th. Had a great deal of rain. Drew one and a half pints of corn meal and half a teaspoonful of salt instead of bread.

2nd day, 6th mo. 6th. I am very weak. Same rations as yesterday. Cloudy all day with some rain. Made souse of the last of our crackers. More prisoners put in today—the place is over crowded.

3rd day, 6th mo. 7th. Had considerable rain. Made a pot of mush which we ate with our meat today. About five hundred more prisoners were put in today.

4th day, 6th mo. 8th. Rain today, same as yesterday. A few more prisoners put in here. I undertook to make a pot of mush this morning; got it about done, when the jaw bone of a hog, which I had it resting on, gave way, and upset the half of it. We made a small breakfast on the remainder. This evening we mixed up some meal and baked some cakes on my plate. Our wood is nearly out. We get corn meal and pork, but are not allowed to go out for wood, and as yet

26

have had none sent to us. My complaint gets no worse, but still sticks to me. Can get no news that can be relied upon.

5th day, 6th mo. 9th. Drew corn bread and had a heavy shower.

6th day, 6th mo. 10th. Was rather warm. Drew bread, meat, and wood. Made coffee for breakfast and supper. Commenced making a bone ring.

7th day, 6th mo. 11th. Was warm, with a thunder gust in the evening. We got to work and finished the bone ring.

1st day, 6th mo. 12th. Cloudy, rain in the afternoon. I am as unwell as ever. Received corn bread and pork. There are many rumors of us being paroled and sent to Savannah. The news is that the officers at Macon are being sent away.

2nd day, 6th mo. 13th. Was very damp and cold, with showers of rain; last night it was also raining. Griffith got sick yesterday and was very ill all last night and today. Had roll-call. All the rumors about the parole have proved untrue. Have suffered much with the chronic diarrhea, which gets no better.

3rd day, 6th mo. 14th. This was a cold drizzly day.

4th day, 6th mo. 15th. Took down our blanket and had it for a cover. It rained all night, and until towards the middle of the day, when it became much warmer. There were over twelve hundred more prisoners put in today from the Army of the Potomac. Sold a loaf of bread and meat for twenty-five cents, and bought an onion and made some soup with it. Had corn meal and pork for supper. Griffith is a little better. An old shoemaker, who has taken the oath of allegiance to the Confederate States, came in today to try to raise one thousand shoemakers, to go out and do as he has, and work for the rebel government. Some of the boys caught him, shaved his head and marched him around camp.

5th day, 6th mo. 16th. There is as much rain as usual. Am getting along in the same old style. Sold a loaf of bread for fifteen cents and bought an onion. Drew boiled rice and meat. The rice is so dirty and gritty that it is not fit to eat. About one thousand more men were put in today, mostly from the Army of the Potomac.

6th day, 6th mo. 17th. Rained all day—lay in the house most of the time. I made some thick corn meal soup for supper. One thousand more prisoners put in today.

7th day 6th mo. 18th. It rained all night and was showery most of the day. My disease is some better—am very weak and losing flesh. The number of petty hucksters seems to increase in the main street. Cucumbers are from 37 to 50 cents; onions from 25 cents to $1.00; turnips from 12 to 20 cents; rutabagas same price as turnips; squashes 25 to 50 cents; peanuts 20 to 25 cents per half pint; beans 25 to 50 cents per half pint; flour at the rate of $1 per pound; four ginger cakes 75 cents to $1; rice 30 to 40 cents per pint; salt 75 cents per quart; soda 25 cents per spoonful; rations of meal for 20 and 25 cents; molasses, of the poorest quality, for $2.75 per quart; tobacco, 50 cents for a small plug. These are offered for sale on the main street at the above prices. A good many have got to making corn beer, at 10 to 25 cents per drink of half a pint. There are rumors that General Winder is here, and that three detachments and all the sick are to be sent away tomorrow.

1st day, 6th mo. 19th. Was up early this morning and went to the spring and got some good water, and washed myself. Took a walk up and down the street, and then lay down and took a good sleep. It was cloudy most of the time. The sun came hot occasionally. Had a heavy shower in the evening. Five hundred more men were put in the stockade today. Three men were shot and wounded by one of the guards. A man was on the *dead-line*; the guard shot at this one, and missing him, shot the others.

2nd day, 6th mo. 20th. Had the usual quantity of rain; was up early and got some spring water.

3rd day, 6th mo. 21st. Was warm and cloudy. I made some coffee and fried some meat on my plate for breakfast—had some gravy also. We did not eat more than half the extra bread we drew last night, and had half a loaf left, which I traded for some wood. A few more prisoners were put in today. The place is so crowded that it is impossible to travel without difficulty.

4th day, 6th mo. 22nd. Was rather cloudy and warm. Drew mush and meat; the mush, like it always has been, was only half cooked; we did not get it until dark, and then went to work and baked it on my plate. Today one hundred men had to fill up a tunnel which they had dug. It was eight to fifteen feet deep and commenced twenty yards inside, and run more than the same distance on the outside, and was ready for them to go out. Some of the crowd had informed on them.

5th day, 6th mo. 23rd. Flying clouds and very hot. There seems to be a good breeze going, but it cannot get to us here. Over seven hundred more prisoners were crowded in today. Drew corn bread and bacon, and would have drawn fresh beef, but some objected to it on account of not having wood.

6th day, 6th mo. 24th. The weather was similar to yesterday, only hotter. Done nothing of any account.

7th day, 6th mo. 25th. Very warm. Drew mush and meat at dark and fried the mush into cakes.

1st day, 6th mo. 26th. The weather like yesterday. Drew the same kind of rations, and fried the mush, because it is never more than half done.

2nd day, 6th mo. 27th. The weather seems to be getting warmer. My diarrhea gets no better—am so weak that I can hardly walk about. There has been enough prisoners put in the last few days to make nearly twenty-five thousand, (25,000).

3rd day, 6th mo. 28th. Had a fine shower this afternoon and night. I am very low and weak with the diarrhea.

4th day, 6th mo. 29th. Was very warm, had a thunder storm in the evening. Am weaker than ever and can hardly get along. Did not get any rations, because some of the men took the "raiders" in hand, and after knocking down, and I guess killed some, arrested sixty and gave them over to the old captain. It is said he shot one. Last night they killed a man, and an Indian killed one of them. I took two bacon rinds and after roasting them by the fire, ate them.

29

5th day, 6th mo. 30th. Was very warm; lay in the tent most of the time; so weak with the chronic diarrhea that it was as much as I could to take care of myself.

6th day 7th mo. 1st. Was as hot as ever. I suffered as much as yesterday; am weaker and still very ill; my head is so dizzy; I could hardly walk. The new stockade was opened this forenoon, and all above the forty-ninth detachment were moved in and crowded close together as we were before. All of us could not put up our shelters in the place allotted to us. Griffith and I made our bed in the street, which is only six feet wide. The new place is on good high ground with plenty of wood. The rumor is that we are to draw raw rations; drew fresh beef and corn meal, of which I ate heartily.

7th day, 7th mo. 2nd. There was a good breeze all day. After I got up, went to the creek and took a wash, got a canteen and coffee pot full of water, and then a little wood. Made the same kind of breakfast as we did supper last night. About eight o'clock moved down with Clark and Strong, [The identity of Clark is undetermined, that of Strong could be Private John Strong, Co. G, 90th P.V. He is listed as a deserter on 7/30/64. It is quite possible he was captured and did not desert. This was the case in a number of other instances in the 90th.] and then crowded nearer the old stockade and towards the lower end of the detachment, and put up our blanket at the end of Strong's tent. All the wood is gathered up by the men, which leaves us with scarcely any. There have been prisoners put in here from all parts this week. Twenty-five thousand is a low estimate. I feel stouter today than I have for two weeks; my complaint hardly troubles me. Drew salt for yesterday and meal, beef, and salt for today. The rumor now is that we will be paroled or exchanged soon, to commence on the 7th, etc., etc. Captain Moore, of the 72nd Ohio, was in here today and gave this piece of news to us. He has been a prisoner at Macon, was lately exchanged, and came here to see some of the boys in his regiment.

30

1st day, 7th mo. 3rd. Griffith and I went to the creek to wash this morning at five o'clock. The creek was dirty and full of black mud, so much so that I would not go in. I took the coffee pot and washed out of it. Got some water and prepared breakfast of beef soup, thickened with corn meal. Had roll—call this forenoon, the first time for three weeks; It was difficult to get the men together, and was eleven o'clock before they got through. Drew no rations today, why I do not know.

2nd day, 7th mo. 4th. Was very hot until three o'clock P.M. when we had a heavy thunder storm. Our house let the rain in almost like a riddle. The numbers of the detachments were changed today; all that were not full were filled up to two hundred and seventy; our detachment is now number thirty—two, and my mess is the second mess. We got no rations until this evening, when we received meal, boiled and raw beef, and pork. Bread and salt were issued; we got raw beef and miserable bread, with a pinch of salt. We made a pot of mush for our breakfast, coffee and stewed meat for supper; we eat only twice a day. My disease has left me and I am stouter. Was down to the creek this morning at four o'clock and took a good wash.

3rd day, 7th mo. 5th. Today was very hot, with a good breeze and flying clouds. Got up this morning at four o'clock, and went to the run and washed my grey shirt and a pair of drawers without soap. We made a pot of soup with corn meal dumplings. Had a roll—call at ten o'clock. Drew meal, fresh beef, and a pinch of salt. Made flap—jacks for supper, and fried some of our beef on my plate. Traded some corn meal for a piece of pork to grease the plate with.

4th day, 7th mo. 6th. Hot as ever. Over two hundred more men put in today. According to rumor, tomorrow is the day to commence paroling. A new rumor says seven thousand are to be taken out tomorrow. Got breakfast of soup off our beef, with corn meal dumplings, and supper of flap—jacks and fried pork. Drew mush, bacon, and salt. *I am very well indeed.*

5th day, 7th mo. 7th. Spent the day as yesterday. No signs of paroling. Very hot today. Fred Smith [Probably Private Fred Smith, Co. G, 90th P.V. who was shown as a deserter in July 1864.] who was taken prisoner near Mine Run, came to see me today. Drew rotten bacon, corn meal, and salt.

6th day, 7th mo. 8th. The heat in the afternoon was almost scorching. I borrowed a book of Hatfield's,[Cannot be further identified.] which I read half through. This is the first reading I have done since we have been here. There were one hundred more men put in today, all of whom were captured at the James and Morris Island.

7th day, 7th mo. 9th. This day was hotter than any day we have had. At four o'clock P.M. had a heavy thunder shower which lasted until sunset. Spent the day in reading, sleeping, and walking about camp. Two hundred and fifty more prisoners put in today. They were mostly from the Potomac Army.

1st day, 7th mo. 10th. Drew rations as usual, consisting of meal, pork, and salt. Cooked flapjacks and made gravy for supper. Our wood is almost out and I know not where the rest will come from; there is plenty in the place, but it is claimed by others. There were six hundred more prisoners put in today from Grant's army.

2nd day, 7th mo. 11th. Hot, with a little shower in the afternoon. Drew meal, salt, and bacon. I had a hard time cooking cakes for breakfast and mush for supper; the wood and roots were too wet. Six of the "raiders" were hung, inside the stockade, by our own men, at five o'clock this evening. The rope of Moseby [Private William Collins, Co. D, 88th P.V.] broke when the drop fell, and let him to the ground; they made him mount the scaffold and try it the second time. One broke loose before he mounted the scaffold and ran through the crowd, but was arrested. [Private Charles Curtis, Battery A, 5th Rhode Island Artillery] I was down helping to draw rations and saw the execution. A large number of prisoners put in today.

32

3rd day, 7th mo. 12th. Was busy most of the day getting wood out of the run, but could not get much. We are out of wood. I made a small furnace to put my plate on. Was running about a great deal—am as well as I could wish to be. There were two hundred more men put in today. I was determined to get an axe to cut some wood, but did not quite get it. I got on the right side of a rebel sergeant, who is a Mason, but he could do no more than ask for me of the one who had charge of the shovels and axes.

4th day, 7th mo. 13th. Very warm. Could get no axe today, but got the promise of one in the morning. Our furnace works first rate. We gathered some roots out of the run, and both of us went down tonight and worked and fished for roots until after ten o'clock. Have got the floor of our tent raised so that water will not flood us.

5th day, 7th mo. 14th. Very hot day. I was up early this morning and down at the run and spring. Got a pot of mush made before roll–call. Got the axe for an hour; we cut enough good pitch pine off a large stump to last us nearly three weeks. Could do little else but lay in the tent after cutting the wood, I was so tired. The diarrhea shows signs of coming on me again. General Winder had the three sergeants of each detachment taken out, and he told them that he knew of an organized gang of six thousand who were going to get out, etc., and the men must not get in crowds within one hundred yards of the gate, or he would fire on them with shot and shell; that they had tried to get us exchanged, but could not, and were compelled to keep us; and that they had plenty to keep us with. I noticed plenty of good looking pies in the market for one dollar and fifty cents watermelons for two and three dollars, and apples for twenty–five and thirty–five cents each.

6th day, 7th mo. 15th. Suffered very much with the diarrhea, which has come back on me as bad as ever.

7th day, 7th mo. 16th. The weather continues to grow hotter. I am some better today; made gruel by soaking corn meal and boiling the water off it. Yesterday drew a ration of wood which was only half enough to cook a meal.

1st day, 7th mo. 17th. The hottest day we have had. I lay in the tent very weak from the diarrhea, which is getting better. Made some corn meal gruel for my breakfast. Drew meat, salt, and molasses, six spoonsful of the latter as a ration. Had flapjacks for supper.

2nd day, 7th mo. 18th. Cloudy and cool all day, with rain in the afternoon, The diarrhea has left me, but I am very weak yet. Had a pot a mush for breakfast. Drew nothing but corn meal today; they issued bacon to some of the detachments, but it did not get to us. Some of the men are trying to get up a petition to be sent to the United States, asking its influence towards getting us released.

3rd day, 7th mo. 19th. Cloudy and pleasant; last night was very cold. Am getting over the diarrhea again. Drew yesterday's pork at nine this forenoon; then got a breakfast of flapjacks, fried pork, and gravy. There was a meeting held today in reference to the petition to our Government for our release. The committee appointed at yesterday's meeting reported. [See Appendix 1, page 52.] General Winder gives his hearty co—operation to the movement and suggests that six instead of three be sent to our government with these petitions, which the meeting took steps to appoint. Last evening I got a pint of beans for five postage stamps, and this morning got a *dagger* for five more.

4th day, 7th mo. 20th. Was up soon after four this morning. Cooked G. Hatfield [Cannot identify further.] a pot of gruel before roll—call; got our own breakfast after roll—call. Washed a pair of drawers and stockings this morning. The rebels threw up some earthworks as if they expected to be attacked. They appear to be getting reinforcements here. The rumor is that the railroad between here and Macon is cut, and that they are expecting a raid by our cavalry, and that Atlanta is ours.

5th day, 7th mo. 21st. Got breakfast after roll—call—had "corn dodgers" and gravy. Drew meal and molasses; got wood for three days. Traded a ration of pork for twenty—five cents worth of wood, and traded a ration of pork for tobacco for Griffith. The rebels seem to be fortifying outside. They put in a few prisoners every day.

6th day, 7th mo. 22nd. Very cloudy and hot. Lay in the house most all the time. Have contracted a cold. More prisoners put in today. The rebels are still busy at their earthworks. They find a tunnel every day and fill it up. Drew meat, salt, and meal.

7th day, 7th mo. 23rd. I caught a bad cold last night, and suffered considerably all day from it. Today the weather was rather cold.

1st day, 7th mo. 24th. Last night was the coldest we have had for some time. My attack of bronchitis has extended far into the chest, and is going to bring on that terrible "army scourge" again. The day was very warm with a good breeze. Drew fresh beef and rice only.

2nd day, 7th mo. 25th. Suffered last night very much with the cold. This night was the coldest yet. The diarrhea has returned and is very bad. The day was warm with a good breeze. Drew rice, bacon, and no salt. I sold a ration of pork and bought two spoonsful of salt.

3rd day, 7th mo. 26th. Was a pleasant day. Made corn meal gruel for breakfast and supper. Borrowed Clark's <u>Infantry Tactics</u> and read and slept all day. Drew meal, salt, and bacon.

4th day, 7th mo. 27th. Was rather pleasant all day. Spent the day as yesterday and drew the same kind of rations. There are a great many rumors about our going to be paroled about the fifth or sixth of next month. There were over two hundred prisoners, mostly one hundred day's men, from the Shenandoah Valley, put in today.

5th day, 7th mo. 28th. Today is pretty warm. Eat nothing but gruel and boiled rice. About two hundred prisoners put in today from Sherman's army. Just as they were ready to enter, the rebels fired a shot across the camp.

6th day, 7th mo. 29th. Today some of the detachments drew molasses; I traded a ration of pork for molasses for supper. Had gruel for breakfast, and boiled rice with the molasses for supper. Today was warm, with a heavy shower in the evening.

7th day, 7th mo. 30th. Was warm. I sold two rations of my meat for twenty-five cents worth of soap, and after roll-call, washed my red shirt. Sold a piece of meat, which Griffith and I had a dispute about, for five cents, and got him a chunk of tobacco.

1st day, 7th mo. 31st. Eat my breakfast and lay in the tent most all day. Am very weak from the diarrhea which I cannot get rid of. J. Matthews [Cannot further identify.] is a prisoner here and has come to see me.

2nd day, 8th mo. 1st. Lay in the tent most of the time. Took a pill which "Gad" got for me tonight; he got one opium and two other pills.

3rd day, 8th mo. 2nd. Took the rest of the medicine today, and think I am better. They commenced taking the sick out and away this morning—suppose they have gone to Macon. During fifteen minutes this evening, we had the heaviest shower I ever saw; Griffith was at the spring and got caught in it. Have been drawing rice, salt, and bacon this week.

4th day, 8th mo. 3rd. They have been busy taking the sick away. Drew meal instead of rice today. Borrowed Roberts' [Cannot further identify.] Bible and read some. Took an opium pill last night which made me sleep until roll-call this morning.

5th day, 8th mo. 4th. Was in the shade under the tent most of the day reading the Bible and getting to sleep. Helped to wash Dr. Buckley this evening; he has been very sick all day. Drew pork and rice. Had no roll-call for the first time since we have been in the new stockade. Some sick were sent out today—rumor says they are being sent into our lines. Today was a warm one.

6th day, 8th mo. 5th. Spent most of the time in the house. Dr. Buckley is some better; we were going to carry him out. The sick of the first eleven detachments were taken out this afternoon. Drew fresh beef, salt, and rice. The diarrhea has left me again; am pretty stout. Ate only rice soup. Occupied in reading the Bible today.

7th day, 8th mo. 6th. Was very hot; lay in the house, slept and read. Drew fresh beef, salt, and a pint of meal.

1st day, 8th mo. 7th. Lay in the tent most of the day, slept and read. Dr. Buckley still keeps poorly.

2nd day, 8th mo. 8th. Had a heavy shower this afternoon. Spent the day as I do most of them. Read almost through Deuteronomy today. Dr. Buckley is no better, but gets worse. Have been drawing fresh beef, meal, and salt. We make soup. Reports are favorable of our being paroled, but as yet we know nothing certain about it. The Quartermaster came in yesterday, and told it around among us, that a parole or exchange was to take place soon, and they were going to commence in a few days.

3rd day, 8th mo. 9th. Was cloudy until about four o'clock this afternoon, when there came up one of the heaviest showers of rain we have had since we came here; it flooded the run and washed some of the stockade above and below, and moved it in several places. They fired off a gun as a signal and out came a large guard. Drew no rations today for our detachment; they ceased to issue after getting to the twentieth. Tried to sell my red shirt, but could not get more than half I asked for it, so I kept it. They have got the frame of a large barracks, large enough for a detachment, at the upper end of the stockade.

4th day, 8th mo. 10th. Rather warm. From 9 A.M. to 3 P.M. had a very hard rain, which did not stop until midnight. We got wet, the tent leaking very badly. Did not draw rations until this morning, when we got beans and half a ration of bread. This evening drew half a ration of bread, salt, and *a very small* ration of beef. Had beef and bean soup for supper; nothing to eat before of any account. I was detailed to draw rations. I carried up a hindquarter of beef. Went and gave Dr. Buckley a sponge bath and washed his shirt in the run.

5th day, 8th mo. 11th. George Hatfield died last night or early this morning. Dr. Buckley is getting better. The "Rebs" have got the stockade almost repaired; they are busy putting up a stockade outside ours. They have some of our boys putting up a barracks near our detachment. Had a heavy rain this afternoon. Did not get

37

our rations until very late; got fresh beef, and a half ration of bread, but no salt.

6th day, 8th mo. 12th. Spent the day reading the Bible and sleeping; it was warm and pleasant. Gave Buckley a sponge bath this afternoon; he is improving rapidly. Have had roll—call the last two mornings. Drew a little meal, a ration of beans, a small ration of beef, and a half ration of salt. They are cutting down the rations. The committee of six which were to go into our lines with the petition, went last First day.

7th day, 8th mo. 13th. Was cloudy most of the time and pleasant. After roll—call, got five others to help to carry Dr. Buckley to the gate to sick call. That the person that Gad sent to attend his man ran off, and we did not get him out. Dr. Buckley fainted twice in our hands; carried him part of the way, and helped him the rest. I washed him this evening—he is better. I am busy reading the Bible. There are many rumors about the parole commencing on the 15th. Drew a ration of beans, and a ration of bread, and fresh beef. We ate only two pots of bean soup. Sold a ration of beef for ten cents and bought two spoonsful of salt.

1st day, 8th mo. 14th. Was a very hot day. Buckley was much worse during the day, but seemed to get better in the evening. I wrote a note to Dr. White, on the outside, asking relief for Buckley, and took it to the Doctor outside, at Doctor's call. Some one told me to put it in the letter box, which I did after consulting two Masons I had found; one belongs to Ohio and the other is a sergeant in the ninety—eight detachment. I washed Buckley this evening. Drew beans, half a ration of beef, and bread, with a little salt. Ate bean soup for breakfast and rice soup for supper. Have the diarrhea.

2nd day, 8th mo. 15th. Spent the day as we did yesterday.

3rd day, 8th mo. 16th. Was very warm, like yesterday. No signs of a parole yet—rumors are all false about it. Have given Buckley a washing every day; he seems to grow better.

38

4th day, 8th mo. 17th. The weather has been extremely warm. Have been drawing half a ration of bread, fresh beef, salt, and beans. I have quit eating beans.

5th day, 8th mo. 18th. Was out and got prescribed for. After the roll—call got six pills; am very weak; am busy reading the Bible. Still give the Doctor a washing every day; he continues to improve.

6th day, 8th mo. 19th. Suffered very much with the diarrhea. Am getting weaker. Went to the Doctor's and got my medicine continued. Did not get any medicine today. Sold my ration of bread and Griffith's for twenty cents and two and a half rations and one of my own for twenty—five cents, which made me twenty cents in cash. Had a heavy rain this evening.

7th day, 8th mo. 20th. Was very warm, with a heavy rain in the evening. Was so weak that I only got out of the tent four times. Buckley was Worse. I was not able to bathe him today.

1st day, 8th mo. 21st. Was in the tent most of the day. Went to the run in the evening and took a bath; gave Dr. Buckley a washing. Had some rain. The Doctor gave me his photograph.

2nd day, 8th mo. 22nd. Very warm. Diarrhea no better—am very weak—lay in the tent most of the day. Buckley is worse, and has a prospect of getting out to the hospital through the influence of his friend Rickers. [Cannot further identify.]

3rd day, 8th mo. 23rd. Drew rice, molasses, and a little pork yesterday; and an old ration of beef, beans, and bread, with a little salt today. Carried Buckley out of the gate at seven o'clock this morning; got him out among the first, but could not get him in the hospital on account of too many being admitted yesterday.

4th day, 8th mo. 24th. About as hot as ever. Went to the Doctor's call and saw Rickers, but there was no chance for Buckley, except by his own surgeon. Have got no medicine for three days. Drew fresh beef, a mouthful of bacon, corn meal, beans, and salt. Ate two rations of beans today, which is going to make me worse. Some of the commissioned—officers, who have been passing off for privates, were taken out today, it is said, to be exchanged. Rumors are favorable for a speedy parole.

5th day, 8th mo. 25th. Did not go to the Doctor's today. Diarrhea something better. Lay in the house most of the day. Bathed Buckley, who is still very low. Drew one–half ration of bread, salt pork, boiled beef, and rice; they are going to give us cooked rations now, and some other detachments raw ones.

6th day, 8th mo. 26th. Very warm. Changed our sergeant of mess by putting out Warner and electing George Suson. [Cannot identify either man further.] Went out to the Doctor's and got prescriptions for Buckley, who has scurvy. My complaint is almost well. The cooked rations agree with me very well. Drew one–half ration of bread, and salt, and a pint of boiled beans, and a ration of molasses. Took a walk over to see Matthews this evening.

7th day, 8th mo. 27th. Was out to the Doctor's call for Buckley. Spent the day in the old way. Drew some extra molasses this forenoon, and boiled rice, beef, pork, and salt for our rations this evening. There was only a mouthful of bacon and the rice only half cooked.

1st day, 8th mo. 28th. Was extremely warm. Spent the day as usual.

2nd day, 8th mo. 29th. Was not well the fore–part of the day and did not get out to the Doctor's. Repeated the vote again for Suson, which elected him, as before. Put Warner in for sergeant of detachment, in place of the sergeant–major, who went out on parole to take charge of ration wagons.

3rd day, 8th mo. 30th. No Doctor's call. Buckley was worse; I bathed him and washed a shirt for him.

4th day, 8th mo. 31st. Washed my drawers this forenoon, and lay about most of the day afterwards. Drew bread, boiled beans, beef, salt, and a bit of bacon. Traded my beef for a ration of beans; ate my beans and pork for supper; traded Griffith's bread for tobacco. Was a warm day.

5th day, 9th mo. 1st. Was out to Doctor's call—no medicine—no prescription. Lay in the house most of the day reading the Bible—

have got through Jeremiah. The news in the Macon Papers is favorable to a speedy exchange. Buckley gets no better. Traded half my bread and beef for beans; ate nothing but a ration and a half of beans for breakfast. Drew the same kind of rations except beans—rice only partly cooked. Last night was so cold that I could not sleep.

6th day, 9th mo. 2nd. Lay in the house—slept and read most all day. Drew the same rations as yesterday—got a piece of pork as large as my fist for a mess of thirty.

7th day, 9th mo. 3rd. Was cloudy and pleasant today. I am rather bad yet. No news about the exchange to be relied on. Griffith has a lame back; complains of the rheumatism.

1st day, 9th mo. 4th. I am very ill indeed; lay quiet all day.

2nd day, 9th mo. 5th. Seemed to be the warmest day; suffered terribly from the heat; lay in the tent most of the day; am very weak. Drew bread, pork, a large ration of molasses, and boiled rice.

3rd day, 9th mo. 6th. My disease is better. Lay in the tent most all day. Eighteen detachments were ordered to be ready to leave at any moment—commencing at the first, going up to the eighteenth.

4th day, 9th mo. 7th. Lay in the tent most of the day and am better. They commenced at the first detachment at seven o'clock this morning and by night got as many as six, and gave orders up as high as eighteen to be ready to leave at a short notice. They ordered at first eighteen detachments to be ready, but could not find transportation for all today. They say they are ordered to Charleston to be exchanged.

5th day, 9th mo. 8th. Lay in the house most of the day. Helped Dr. Buckley all I could. Drew beans, boiled beef, salt, and corn meal. They send off prisoners as fast as they can get transportation; have not got more than twenty detachments away yet; they took some of the higher detachments after getting up to the eighteenth—seventy-six to eighty. Matthews got off.

6th day, 9th mo. 9th. Was extremely warm today. Helped to carry Buckley up to the barracks; was busy waiting on him until near noon; he is very ill; at noon he was admitted to the hospital; I went outside the gate with him; the rebel sergeant would not allow me to stay out with him. The barracks were vacated and filled up with the sick of the detachments which have left. The Drs. commenced and admitted large numbers to the hospital. I have diarrhea very bad. About two thousand men were taken away; they ship them off as fast as they can.

7th day, 9th mo. 10th. Had a severe spell of chills and fever last night; being so bad the day before was the cause of it; drank plenty of water, which soon stopped the chills, and threw me into a fever. Was so weak today, could hardly go about. About the same number as yesterday were sent off; they mostly started in the night. Drew bread, boiled rice, molasses, and salt.

1st day, 9th mo. 11th. This was a very warm day. There was not so many got away except this morning. About all the old prisoners are gone. Yesterday evening, all from 19 to 23 were ordered to be ready. About three o'clock this afternoon, all from 23 to 33 were ordered to be ready. No sooner was the order given than the "boys" packed up and moved off to the gate. Each detachment took up its position ready to go. Here we lay, anxiously waiting for the cars to come, which were expected at five o'clock, but they did not come. We lay down on the ground. Drew boiled rice this forenoon. After getting to the gate, got boiled beef. I am some better, but so weak and thin, I can just get along. Griffith has such a lame back, he cannot get along much better than I.

2nd day, 9th mo. 12th. We lay ready to go until almost five o'clock. Drew rice, molasses, and bread, for two days rations. I am very weak, hardly able to walk. At five the trains began to come in; we moved out and got in the cars; sixty to a car. About six o'clock they gave us two days rations of corn bread and pork; started about dusk and arrived at Macon about the middle of the night.

42

3rd day, 9th mo. 13th. Lay in the cars until daylight; then started and got to Augusta by evening; stopped there about two hours, then changed cars and started again about dusk.

4th day, 9th mo. 14th. Kept on all night, going on the Columbia road, and came to a junction which went to Charleston; and, at noon, came to another junction, one leading towards Wilmington, which we took, after changing cars, and started about five o'clock, and continued going on pretty steady all night.

5th day, 9th mo. 15th. Arrived at a village called Florence, South Carolina, and encamped here. Arrived here about two o'clock last night; lay in the cars until eleven o'clock today, then were moved out about a mile from the place. Clark, Joice, Griffith, and I, put up a snug tent of two blankets. The day, and, in fact, the weather has been very warm since we started; we are almost worn out.

6th day, 9th mo. 16th. Slept very cold last night; have the diarrhea very bad, and am so weak that I can hardly go about; did not get any rations until twelve o'clock at night, and then only a pint of meal and a little piece of pork. The rebel Captain called the roll this evening. The camp is divided into messes of one hundred, and detachments of three thousands. I am in mess sixth of our detachment.

7th day, 9th mo. 17th. Was a very warm day; I got no better; am so weak can hardly help myself. Last night was so cold I could not sleep, until we took down the blankets and put them over us. Drew a pint of rice for two days rations.

1st day, 9th mo. 18th. Drew a pint of beans, pork, and salt. Had roll—call; all that were sick and not able to go were excused; and, after roll—call, were ordered to the hospital. I was put on the sick list. About noon we were taken outside of the camp for the purpose of drawing better rations. In the evening drew a good ration of sweet potatoes, a leaf of cabbage, a little beef, and salt. I have Griffith's overcoat, which is the only shelter I have. Close, Roberts, Clark, and I are together.

2nd day, 9th mo. 19th. Lay under our tree, and sit by the fire all night; it was very cool. Drew same rations as yesterday, excepting the cabbage; got a square inch of pumpkin. About noon got orders to move to the opposite side of the camp, when the most able men, the nurses, and those who wished, were sent back to camp; the rest put in detachments of one hundred. I am in the seventh detachment; are in the woods, with water handy.

3rd day, 9th mo. 20th. Had a cool night of it last night; lay in the woods until five o'clock; then were taken up to the shedding in the field. Clark and I went back to the woods to sleep. It was cloudy all night and in the evening rained. Drew same rations as yesterday.

4th day, 9th mo. 21st. Lay under our tree all night and were up at daylight; had a cold night of it. The nurses put up some boughs over poles for us, but they made poor shelter, excepting from the sun. We were worse off here excepting the rations. Drew a sweet potato, five spoonfuls of flour, the same of rice, and a half tablespoonful of salt. My diarrhea is almost checked, but my strength is poor yet.

5th day, 9th mo. 22nd. It rained last night but I lay in my overcoat and kept dry. Drew the same rations of flour as yesterday, two spoonsful of corn meal, rice, salt, and a mouthful of bacon. Make gruel and rice soup mostly for Close and I. Am decidedly better today. Had a good deal of rain this evening.

6th day, 9th mo. 23rd. Was cloudy all day; rained in the fore-part of the night; made out to sleep a little. Got some dead pine leaves and spread on the ground for my bed. My overcoat kept me from getting "wringing wet." Got everything dry today, and went to the creek and took a bath. All who were able were sent to the creek to bathe, and before they got back the doctor sent three hundred and fifty of them back to camp. I cannot gain strength. Drew hominy, rice, flour, and a pinch of salt.

7th day, 9th mo. 24th. Lay about all day and cooked. had a heavy rain in the evening. Drew corn meal, rice, fresh beef, and a pinch of salt. My old complaint is back on me as bad as ever.

44

1st day, 9th mo. 25th. Was a clear, warm, and windy day. My diarrhea gets no better. Drew fresh beef, a good ration, and salt only. Made soup of rice. I cook for Close. All who could walk were sent back to camp; I was left out, being able to walk only a little. Clark was sent in. Had a cool night.

2nd day, 9th mo. 26th. Last night was very cold—cold enough for frost. Today was fine and clear, but rather cool. Am very weak and prostrated. There are some rumors of an exchange going on.

3rd day, 9th mo. 27th. Was warm; last night was cold. All excepting the worst cases were sent to camp. I got some medicine this evening—a pill of camphor and opium; some with dysentery got oleum rieni and spirits of turpentine. The scurvy cases, a concoction of sumac berries, which was pleasant to drink. Some kind citizens sent some boiled sweet potatoes, ham, cabbage, and bread for the worst cases. The steward, who seems to notice me considerably, gave Close and I some of the above named articles, so we wanted no supper. Drew corn meal, fresh beef, and salt. I cooked beans until eleven o'clock at night for our breakfast. Am no better, but have a good appetite.

4th day, 9th mo. 28th. Was very warm all day; spent the day as yesterday. Drew meal, beans, and salt.

5th day, 9th mo. 29th. Was a warm night; I slept well. My complaint is no better; am very weak. Drew meal, rice, salt, molasses, and some sweet potatoes; the molasses is of the worst sorghum. They give us medicine once per day.

6th day, 9th mo. 30th. Spent the day laying in my shed. My disease is on the mend. Got to the creek and took a bath this forenoon. Drew fresh beef, rice, meal, and salt. Got medicine today. The men die pretty fast.

7th day. 10th mo. 1st. Lay quiet as possible. Drew one half of a large hard tack, eight spoonsful of molasses, and salt.

1st day, 10th mo. 2nd. Was busy pottering around all day. Drew one half of hard tack, eight spoonsful of molasses, salt, corn meal, and flour. The men are dying off very fast all around me. Griffith was put in the third ward. Got my cap and gum blanket.

2nd day, 10th mo. 3rd. Spent the day as yesterday. Had some rain in the evening. Drew fresh beef, beans, flour, and salt. My health is better.

3rd day, 10th mo. 4th. Lay quiet; my complaint is some better. Drew molasses, rice, flour, and salt—a good ration.

4th day, 10th mo. 5th. Lay quiet. Took a dose of olium vicini last night. Did not eat much today; am getting stouter. Drew meal, beans, and salt. Was a warm and pleasant day. Edward Roberts died in the afternoon. I went down to see how he was, and found him only breathing.

5th day, 10th mo. 6th. Am getting better; walked around a good deal today. Sold my knife for six dollars in Confederate money; also five pearl buttons for fifty cents, Partly cooked some beans after ten o'clock this evening. Had a heavy rain.

6th day, 10th mo. 7th. Am better today than I have been for some time. Bought seven sweet potatoes for fifty cents and ate half of them. Drew fifteen small crackers, sent to us by the Sanitary Commission, and some flour and salt. Wrote a letter for Close to his father; he has given up all hopes of recovery.

7th day, 10th mo. 8th. Was clear and cool all day. Drew fifteen small crackers, a small spoonful of beef tea, some condensed milk, and coffee. Two rations made only a pint of coffee; I gave all to Close—he seemed to relish them. Shirts and drawers were issued to those who needed them; they were sent by the Sanitary Commission. I feel better and stouter today, and made out to draw three buckets of water and carry it. Sold a knife for Close for one dollar, and bought one dollar's worth of sweet potatoes.

1st day, 10th mo. 9th. Was very cool all day. Drew the usual rations. The men are dying off very fast.

2nd day, 10th mo. 10th. Last night it was so cold that it was as much as I could do to keep from freezing. It was clear and cool all day. Drew thin half blankets for those who had none, also socks and drawers, from the Sanitary Commission.

3rd day, 10th mo. 11th. Spent the day, which was very cool, as yesterday. Drew the same kind of rations.

4th day, 10th mo. 12th. Was warm today. Have been troubled with a sore mouth, arising from a bad cold. Medicine does no good. Drew medicine, got drowsy and went to bed.

5th day, 10th mo. 13th. Have had a worse attack of that "terrible scourge" today than I have had for a long time. Took medicine to no purpose.

6th day, 10th mo. 14th. I am no better; worse if anything. Drew "Sanitary stuff" for the worst cases, and fresh beef, flour, and corn meal.

7th day, 10th mo. 15th. Was a fine day; lay quiet most of the time. Sanitary stuff for Close, and the worst cases were issued. Drew some crackers with a ration. Put Close's and mine in a soup. My complaint seems to be better.

1st day, 10th mo. 16th. A pleasant day. Close about the same. Drank concentrated coffee and sconce. I feel better but cannot get my disease checked. Took three cathartic pills this evening. Drew no rations.

2nd day, 10th mo. 17th. Was the same kind of day today as others. Close was worse all day; the ward—master got him an egg, some beef tea, and coffee, which he ate and yet seemed hungry. We think he cannot live over night.

3rd day, 10th mo. 18th. Covered Close up with all the blankets, and got permission to sleep by the nurse's fire. The night was cool. Close kept sinking until four o'clock this morning, when he died. It looks like rain again this morning. Burns, one of the nurses, and I, put up a tent of my gum blanket and one of the new blankets. I am not much better.

4th day, 10th mo. 19th. Warm and pleasant; was busy most of the time, but did not do much. The Sanitary Commission has been sending clothing here, but it is rather light stuff, such as red pants, gray drawers, and red and gray shirts.

47

5th day, 10th mo. 20th. Lay as quiet as possible all day. Am better.

6th day, 10th mo. 21st. Lay as quiet as possible all day. The nights are very cool.

7th day, 10th mo. 22nd. Last night was very cool, but I got a good night's rest. Today was blustery and cold, but clear. At ten o'clock the hospital was moved inside of the stockade, and to the northwest corner of it. All who were able to walk were sent ahead, and after getting in were taken across the creek and put in charge of a corporal. I took a walk around and bought two Confederate dollars worth of sweet potatoes for my dinner; traded all my beans for salt; then took a walk to the hospital grounds, and found our steward and nurses, who told me to bring my things. Burns and I put up a tent as before and prepared for a cold night; ate a little boiled rice. The steward gave me four spoonsful of canned tomatoes and a biscuit for my supper.

1st day, 10th mo. 23rd. Was cool; lay about, and kept warm in the sun and the tent.

2nd day, 10th mo. 24th. Lay in the tent most of the time. A Mason, ward master, came to see me. A rebel Lieutenant was looking around for us. The back of my hands are so badly chapped I can hardly do anything.

It appears that from inability or some other cause, Charles Smedley was unable to give us any further account of his trials and sufferings; and that the 24th of the 10th month, 1864, was the last day he was able to write. I have deemed it appropriate to add the following account of his last days(obtained from Richard Dobbins, who was the steward or wardmaster, referred to by Charles, and who attended him until near his last moments,) as a finale to his own history, as given in his diary.

                                        Joel Smedley

Having had some acquaintance with Charles Smedley—the writer of the foregoing diary—for some time previous to his decease, at the request of his father, I shall endeavor to give some account, from memory, of the last days of his existence; also, a brief account of my own experience while in the hands of the rebels, as their prisoner.

My name is Richard Dobbins, a native of western Missouri. I belonged to Company H, 18th Regiment Iowa Volunteers—was taken prisoner at the Battle of Missionary Ridge, November 25th, 1863—was sent to the Libby Prison, in Richmond, Virginia, where I remained a short time. Then I was sent to Belle Island, where I suffered very much from cold and starvation. I often thought of death, which stared me in the face daily; though I was not worse off than the majority of the other prisoners. I remained there until the 16th of March, 1864, when I was sent with others to Andersonville, in Georgia, where I suffered very much; not so much from starvation as on the island, but from rain and cold; also from smoke, from the burning of pine wood. We were of course thinly clad, some destitute of blankets, some of shoes, some of pants, while others had scarcely any clothes on them. The majority of us had been searched and robbed of all our good clothing, money, watches, etc. It seemed as though we could expect nothing but death to relieve us from our sufferings. Over twelve thousand of the prisoners died at Andersonville.

On the 8th of September, I, with others, was sent from there, and in due time arrived at Savannah. From thence we were moved to Charleston, South Carolina, where the rebels made a kind of military display of us, by marching us through the city, and putting us in prison, near the officers who were under the fire of our guns.

We remained there only one day and night, and then were marched to the rear of the city, on the race—course track, where we staid but a short time; then I was sent to Florence, South Carolina. Shortly after I arrived there, I was taken out on "parole of

49

Above shows a panoramic view of the interior of the Andersonville stockade. A.J. Riddle, a southern photographer, took this photograph, and the one on the opposite page on August 17th, 1864.

Another panoramic view, this shows the northern prison camp at Elmira, N.Y. Although the squlor of the southern camps is not evident, the death rate was 5% per month.

Riddle's photographs were taken in August 1864 when the stockade at Andersonville was filled with 33,000 prisoners.

The rebels in the Elmira stockade dubbed it "Hellmira." Thousands of Confederate enlisted men died needlessly in this and other northern camps.

Another Riddle view of the stockade interior at Andersonville clearly shows the squalid conditions inside the camp.

This scene shows the sinks running beside the stream which provided the only source of drinking water to the camp. The resulting contamination contributed to thousands of deaths.

An artist's portrayal of the stockade at Andersonville. This view exaggerates the overcrowded conditions inside the stockade, making it appear even more crowded than it was.

A postwar view of the camp shows the remains of the gateway to the stockade. More than 13,000 passed through only to find death inside.

A burial detail is shown placing dead prisoners in the long
trenches used to contain the large numbers of prisoners who died
each day inside the stockade.

A large piece of the stockade wall has survived to the present day. This piece is about four feet high and is part of the collection of the G.A.R. Museum in Philadelphia.

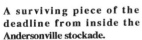

A surviving piece of the deadline from inside the Andersonville stockade.

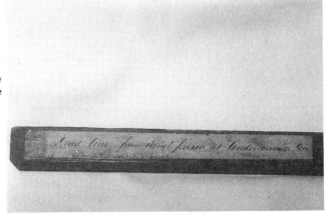

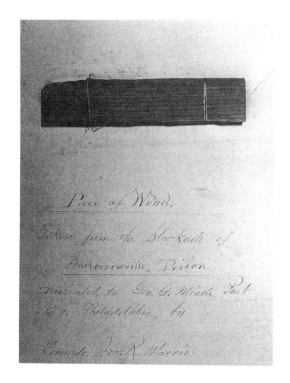

Several other smaller pieces of the Andersonville stockade recovered by Union veterans and donated to the G.A.R. Museum in Philadelphia.

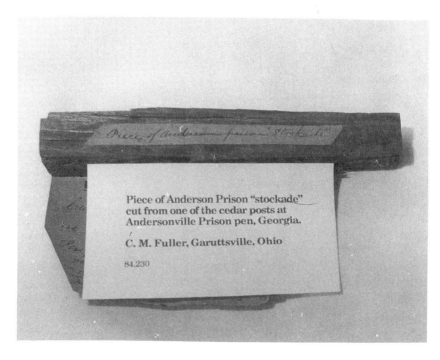

Piece of Anderson Prison "stockade" cut from one of the cedar posts at Andersonville Prison pen, Georgia.

C. M. Fuller, Garuttsville, Ohio

84.230

A scene from better times, this 1863 lithograph shows Union prisoners of war playing baseball inside the prison camp at Salisbury, North Carolina. Unfortunately, by the time the men of the 90th Pennsylvania arrived in Salisbury between May and August 1864, this scene was a faded memory. More than 4,000 prisoners died in the overcrowded camp by the end of the war.

A number of items exhibited as "Andersonville relics." Many of the items were made to assist the prisoners in preparing and serving their food.

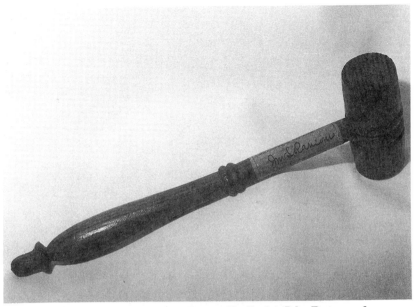

A gavel carved by another Andersonville diarist, John Ransom of the 9th Michigan Cavalry.

The steamer, Sultanna, was transporting almost 2,000 recently exchanged prisoners of war. On April 17, 1865, a few miles above Memphis, one of the ship's boilers exploded. Some soldiers were killed immediately in the explosion, others died in the fire which followed while still others drowned. More than 1,500 soldiers died in this tragic accident. The incident inflamed existing passions of northerners who wanted revenge for perceived southern atrocities against prisoners of war.

This view of the ragged prisoners and their makeshift shelters provides a clear understanding of the terrible death rate inside the stockade.

Scenes like these, and the descriptions of them by surviviors of the camp, helped to fuel the northern outrage at the end of the war. The United States Government made attempts to procure evidence of a southern conspiracy to kill prisoners. Such evidence was never found.

This photograph shows the interior of the stockade with the "deadline" clearly visible in the lower right corner. The prisoner's shelters are built right up to the line.

An 1884 lithograph depicts a guard shooting a prisoner for crossing the "deadline."

The graves of the six Andersonville raiders who were tried and found guilty of murder. They were hanged on July 11, 1864. Charles Smedley witnessed their execution.

A postwar view of the deteriorating stockade shows log pillars rotting and crumbling to the ground.

This view shows the postwar remains of the numerous wells dug by the inhabitants of the stockade.

Some of the 13,000 Union graves are shown above in the postwar cemetery.

The site of "Providence Spring" which appeared after a part of the stockade wall collapsed during the second week of August 1864. The inmates of the stockade viewed it as evidence of Divine intervention in their behalf.

General John Winder, the Commissary General of prisoners of war for the Confederacy, may have been the man the prisoners hated more than any other of their captors.

The result of the outrage in the North over the "atrocities" in Andersonville was the trial and execution of Henry Wirz, the stockade commander. His trial was a farce. The outcome was a foregone conclusion. The United States executed Henry Wirz on November 10, 1865. His execution is documented in these two photographs.

Reporters gather to witness the execution of the "monster," Henry Wirz, the "butcher of Andersonville."

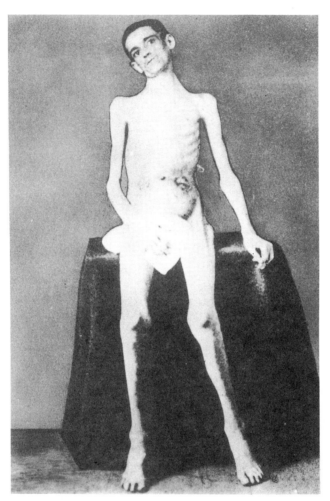

Charles Smedley wrote, "There are men here just like skeletons."
He did not exaggerate. Unfortunately, this is not the worst
photograph of Andersonville survivors.

The Pennsylvania Monument at Andersonville pays tribute to the approximately 1800 Pennsylvanians who died there.

A bronze marker from the Pennsylvania Monument shows prisoners dipping for water from a spring on the far side of the deadline.

A sketch of the gates of the Andersonville stockade, which was
drawn shortly after the prison ceased operation.

State of Pennsylvania
County of Lancaster } ss:

On this Tenth day of April, A.D. 1867, personally appeared before me, the Prothonotary of the Court of Common Pleas in and for the County and State aforesaid, Joel Smedley, of Fulton township, in the County and State aforesaid, aged sixty-seven years, who being affirmed declares that he is the father of Charles Smedley, late of the township, County and State aforesaid, who was a corporal in Co. "G" of the 90th Regt Pa Vols, who died in the service of the United States at Florence, North Carolina, about the 15th day of November, 1864, leaving neither wife nor child; that the mother of the deceased soldier died on the 5th day of November, 1863, and that he has never been engaged in any way in, aided or abetted the Rebellion in the United States.

Joel Smedley

A sworn statement alleged to have been filed by Joel Smedley, father of Charles Smedley, in an application for a survivor's pension. It was an attempt to defraud the Government.

Fulton 2mo. 11th '/70

Commissioner of Pensions,

A series
of documents, dated ~~dated~~ Dec. 25th '69
relative to a pension, was received a
few days since, by me, — I submitted the
papers, to my "Attorney" Daniel G. Baker Esq.
of Lancaster, for his advice in the matter, —
he replied by saying, "I have examined the
papers sent you by the Pension Office, —
There must be some mistake about it,
I never sent any papers for you, for a
pension, and never received any from Wash
=ington in relation to such a claim, — I knew
you were not a "dependant" father, that
you were not entitled to a pension, and
~~therefore~~ never made application, —
It is possible, that some rascal has
been using your name for the purpose
of swindling the Government." —
"I think it would be well for you to

In response to papers received from the Government, Joel Smedley's lawyer advised, "It is possible that some rascal has been using your name for the purpose of swindling the Government."

send Letter No 14, back to the Commission
-er, with a note, stating that you never
made application, and were not entitled
to a pension", ——— I have a faint
recollection, of having received a commun
=nication from the department, relating to
a pension, some two years since, but knowing
I was not entitled to a pension, thought it
not necessary to answer it, ——

Should any person have made
Application in my name, on account
of the "Soldier, Charles Smedley, who was
my Son, and who died in the Rebel prison
at Florence, South Carolina, you may
consider it as fraudulent, —

Very Respectfully &c.
Joel Smedley
Fulton House P. O,
Lancaster County,
Pa —

**A letter from Joel Smedley informing the Government that any
pension request filed in his name was an attempt to defraud the
United States.**

honor," and sent to the Federal hospital by the rebel surgeons, as master of one of the wards there.

It was there I became acquainted with Corporal Charles Smedley, of Company G, Ninetieth Regiment Pennsylvania Volunteers,(although I had frequently seen him at sick call while at Andersonville, but did not make his acquaintance,) who was a patient at my ward.

A little incident occurred there that manifested his kind and generous disposition, which attracted my attention, and caused me to feel deep interest in his welfare. I had prepared some food for him, the best I could get, and took it to him. He immediately gave it all to David Close,(who was a fellow prisoner with him, and very sick,) saying, "You need it worse than I."

When he first came to the hospital, he complained of chronic diarrhea and dysentery. After a few days the dysentery left him, though he was still very weak. He kindly waited on David Close, and seemed willing to do all he could for him, as he considered Close worse than himself. I think he hurt himself by over exertion. He waited on Close all he could, until he died, which appears to have occurred on the morning of 18th of October.

A few days after the death of David Close, the hospital was moved inside of the stockade, to the northwest corner. Charles, with others, walked in. In the evening Charles came over to the hospital. We told him he had better get his things, and come back to the hospital and stay, which he did. Shortly after he came, his hands became very sore, apparently from a dropsical affection, and were bandaged up.

His walk, from the hospital to the inside of the stockade, appeared to have been too much for his strength. From that day he became worse, though he was able to walk about, almost every day, until the day before he died.

He gave me his watch some time before, saying, "I might drop off at any time," and requested me, if it should so happen, to take it home to his father, and tell him all, which I promised him I would do, if it was possible. He seemed cheerful, and manifested no fears of death. In fact, he always appeared cheerful and in

50

good spirits, and seemed confident that he would get home again. He certainly had a very hard and trying time while in prison, but seldom heard to complain or find fault. *He was a good soldier and a true patriot.*

He died on the night of the 16th of November 1864. He was washed, shaved, and clean clothes put on him, but no coffin was provided for him. His body was wrapped in a sheet and buried in a burial ground, a short distance north of north–west of the stockade. The number of his grave was probably recorded at the rebel headquarters, as is their custom, but I do not know the number. I tried to get the number, but could not, for reasons best known to the rebel officers.

After his death I secured his Bible, diary, a small book in which he kept the photographs of his family, and a few little tools, with which he used to while away the time in making bone rings, etc.; all of which, with the watch, according to my promise, I have succeeded in delivering to his father.

I was paroled on the 29th of November, 1864, and sent from Florence, South Carolina, to Savannah, Georgia, where I was put on shipboard, and brought, with many others, to Annapolis, Maryland, where I arrived on the morning of the 5th of December, and immediately informed Charles Smedley's father of his sad fate.

Richard Dobbins, Co.H, 17th Iowa Volunteers.

Appendix 1

Prisoner's Petition to the United States Government

At a meeting of the sergeants in charge of the various detachments of prisoners confined at Andersonville, Georgia, held for the purpose of taking some action to properly represent the present conditions of the prisoners to our Government at Washington, and thereby secure, if possible, a speedy redress of the wrongs complained of, the following committee was appointed, who, after due consultation, reported the following preamble and resolutions, which were unanimously adopted:

Committee.—*William W. Johnson, chairman; H.C. Higginson, J.S. Banks, E.W. Webb.*

Preamble.—Apparently one of the sad effects of the progress of this terrible war has been to deaden our sympathies and make us more selfish than we were when the tocsin of battle strife first sounded in the land. Perhaps this state of public feeling was to have been anticipated. The frequency with which you hear of captures in battle, and the accounts which you have seen of their treatment, has robbed the spectacle of its novelty and, by a law of our nature, has taken off the edge of sensibilities and made them less the object of interest. No one can know the horrors of imprisonment in crowded and filthy quarters but him who has endured it, and it requires a brave heart not to succumb. But hunger, filth, nakedness, squalor, and disease are as nothing compared with the heartsickness which wears prisoners down, most of them young men whose terms of enlistment have expired, and many of them with nothing to attach them to the cause in which they suffer but principle and love of country and friends. Does this misfortune of being taken prisoner make us less the object of interest and value to our Government? If such you plead, plead it no longer. These

52

are no common men, and it is no common merit that they call upon you to aid in their release from captivity.

We, undersigned sergeants in the U.S. Army, having in charge the various detachments of prisoners now confined in Andersonville, Georgia would respectfully represent:

First. That a large portion of the prisoners have been held as such for periods from nine to fifteen months, subject to all hardships and privations incident to a state of captivity in an enemy's country.

Second. That there are now confined in this prison from 25,000 to 30,000 men, with daily accessions of hundreds, and that the mortality among them, generated by various causes, such as change of climate, dirt, the want of proper exercise, is becoming truly frightful to contemplate, and is rapidly increasing to virulence, decimating their ranks by hundreds weekly.

Third. In view of the foregoing facts we, your petitioners, most earnestly yet respectfully pray that some action be immediately taken to effect our speedy release, either on parole or by exchange, the dictates both of humanity and justice alike demanding it on the part of the Government.

Fourth. We shall look forward with hopeful confidence that something will be speedily done in this matter, believing that a proper statement of the facts is all that is necessary to secure a redress of grievances complained of.

Fifth. The above has been read to each detachment by its respective sergeant and been approved by the men, who have unanimously authorized each sergeant to sign it as will and deed of the whole.

This petition was signed by the detachment sergeants, more than one hundred of them and forwarded to the United States government along with the following letter.

Camp Sumter, Andersonville, Georgia   July 20 1864

In order to facilitate the circulation of the enclosed petition we would respectfully urge the necessity of having representatives from the prisoners here confined, who will be permitted to convey within the U.S. lines and place before the people, through the medium of the Associated Press of the United States, also the Governors of the respective states, and to the Executive authority of the United States, the facts contained in the accompanying documents, and to do whatever may be advisable in reference thereto. Believing as we do that such a course would best subserve the ends in view, we as a committee of the whole, respectfully submit the following named persons, subject to your approval, to consummate the undertaking: Edward Bates, Company K, 42nd New York; H.C. Higginson, Company K, 19th Illinois; S. Noirot, William N. Johnson, F. Garland; Prescot Tracy, Company G, 82nd New York.

S. Noirot

Chairman.

C.A. Mc Claskey,

Secretary for Committee.

Office of the Provost Marshal General,

Department of the South,

Hilton Head, South Carolina, August 19, 1864

Prescott Tracey, private Company G, 82nd New York Volunteers, from New York City, a prisoner of war, captured at Petersburg on the 22nd of June; from Petersburg was taken to Richmond; from Richmond to Belle Island. Over 1,200 men were at Belle Island; we were starved there; our treatment was very bad. From Belle Island we were taken to Lynchburg; thence we marched seventy-five miles to Danville; it took five days, and all we had to eat was a few crackers, from eleven to fifteen for each man for the trip. At

Danville we were well treated.   From Danville we went to Andersonville, and were nearly starved to death; we had no shelter; they stole our blankets, money, coffee, and everything; we were completely robbed. On the road down some of the officers made the men take rings off their fingers. Most of the men at Andersonville are nearly naked; they steal the clothing off your back; they stole my shirt, the only one I had; they made me take it off.

Some of the men have no clothing except a meal—bag with a hole cut for their head and others for their arms, their clothing having been all stolen.

We have no shelter whatever from sun, rain, or cold; no covering at night. Full one half are sick with malignant diarrhea and scurvy, the worst and most loathsome kind. There are some 34,672 prisoners there; from 80 to 145 die daily. We find them lying dead all over the camp in the morning. The hospital department is outside the stockade, with a few tents, but most of the men are on the ground without bed or shelter. The surgeons, as a general rule, are kind, and do what they can, but they have no medicine and very little means of doing for the sick.

The petition inclosed was suggested by some of the rebel sergeants who call the roll; they asked why we did not get up a petition to our Government. The authorities gave us the paper, and it was agreed, if we would tell nothing but the truth, it would be forwarded to the rebel Government and thence to Washington, to endeavor to effect a parole. I was one of the committee. I desire to be permitted to go to Washington, together with three men, Bates, Higginson, and Noirot, and personally represent the case to the President. The statement was got up so as to pass the rebel authorities; it does not tell a tithe, no, not a thousandth part of our miseries...

The petition which Prescott Tracey delivered was not acted on by the Lincoln Administration. Little was done by the Federal

Government to alleviate the suffering of the Prisoners in Andersonville.

Appendix 2

Inspection Report
Assistant Adjutant & Inspector
General
Colonel D.T. Chandler
Andersonville Prison

Anderson, July[August] 5, 1864.

Colonel R. H. Chilton,

Assistant Adjutant and Inspector General, Richmond;

Colonel: Having, in obedience to instructions of 25th of July ultimo, carefully inspected the Federal prisoners of war and post at this place, I respectfully submit the following report:

The Federal prisoners of war are confined within a stockade 15 feet high, of roughly hewn pine logs about 8 inches in diameter, inserted 5 feet into the ground, inclosing, including the recent extension, an area of 540 by 260 yards. A railing around the inside of the stockade and about 20 feet from it constitutes the "dead line," beyond which the prisoners are not allowed to pass, and about 3 and 1/4 acres near the center of the inclosure are so marshy as to be at present unfit for occupation, reducing the available present area to about 23 and 1/2 acres, which gives somewhat less than 6 square feet to each prisoner. Even this is being constantly reduced by the additions to their number. A small stream passes from west to east through the inclosure at about 150 yards from its southern limit and furnishes the only water for washing accessible to the prisoners. Some regiments of the guard, the bakery, and the cook house, being placed on the rising of the stream before it enters the prison, render the water nearly unfit for use before it reaches the prisoners. This is now being remedied in part by the removal of the cook–house. Under the pressure of their necessities the prisoners have dug numerous wells within the inclosure, from which they obtain an ample supply of water to drink of good quality. Excepting the edges of this stream, the soil is sandy and easily drained, but from 30 to 50 yards on each side of it the ground is a muddy marsh, totally unfit for occupation, and having been constantly used as a sink since the prison was first established, it is now in shocking condition and cannot fail to breed pestilence. An effort is being made by Captain Wirz, commanding the prison, to fill up the marsh and construct a sluice—the upper end to be used for bathing, etc., the lower as a sink—but the difficulty of procuring lumber and tools very much retards the work and threatens soon to stop it. No shelter whatever, nor materials for constructing any, has been provided by the prison authorities, and the ground being entirely bare of trees, none is within reach of the prisoners, nor has it been possible, from the overcrowded state of the inclosure, to arrange the camp with any system. Each man has been permitted to protect himself the best he can, stretching his blanket, or whatever he may have, above him on such sticks as he can procure, thatches of pine or whatever his ingenuity may suggest and his cleverness supply. Of other, there is and has been none. The whole number of prisoners is divided into messes of 270, and subdivisions of 90 men, each under a sergeant of their own number and selection, and but one C.S. officer, Captain Wirz, is assigned to the supervision and control of the whole. In consequence of this fact and the absence of all regularity in the prison grounds, and there being no barracks or tents, there are and can be no regulations established for the "police consideration for the health, comfort, and sanitary condition of those within the inclosure," and none are practicable under existing circumstances.

In evidence of their condition I would cite the facts that numbers have been found murdered by their comrades, and that recently, in their desperate efforts to provide for their own safety; a court organized among themselves, by authority of General Winder, commanding the post, granted on their own application, has tried a large number of their fellow prisoners and sentenced six to be hung, which sentence was duly executed by themselves within the stockade, with the sanction of the post commander. His order in the case has been forwarded by him to the War Department. There is no medical attendance furnished within the stockade. Small quantities of medicines are placed in the hands of certain prisoners of each squad or division, and the sick are directed to be brought out by the sergeants or squads daily at "sick call" to the medical officers who attend at the gate. The crowd at these times is so great that only the strongest can get access to the doctors, the weaker ones being unable to force their way through the press; and the hospital accommodations are so limited that, though the beds(so called) have all nearly two occupants each, large numbers who would otherwise be received are necessarily sent back to the stockade. Many—twenty yesterday—are carted out daily, who have died from unknown causes and whom the medical officers have never seen. The dead are hauled out daily by the wagonload and buried without coffins, their hands in many instances being first mutilated with an ax in the removal of any finger rings they may have. The sanitary condition of the prisoners is as wretched as can be, the principal causes of mortality being scurvy and chronic diarrhea, the percentage of the former being disproportionately large among those brought from Belle Isle. Nothing seems to have been done, and but little, if any effort, made to arrest it by procuring proper food. The ration is one third pound of bacon and one pound and a quarter unbolted corn meal, with fresh beef at rare intervals, and occasionally rice. When to be obtained—very seldom—a small quantity of molasses is substituted for the meat ration. A little weak vinegar, unfit for use, has sometimes been issued. The arrangements for cooking and baking have been wholly inadequate, and though additions are now being completed it will still be impossible to cook for the whole number of prisoners. Raw rations have to be issued for a very large proportion who are entirely unprovided with proper utensils and furnished so limited a supply of fuel they are compelled to dig with their hands in the filthy marsh before mentioned for roots, etc. After inquiry I am confident that by slight exertions green corn and other antiscorbutics could readily be obtained. Herewith I hand two reports of Chief Surgeon White, to which I respectfully call your attention. The present hospital arrangements were only intended for the accommodation of the sick of 10,000 men, and are totally insufficient, both on character and extent, for the present needs; the number of prisoners being more now than three times as great, the number of cases requiring medical treatment is in an increased ratio. It is impossible to state the number of sick, many dying within the stockade whom the medical officers never see or hear of 'till their remains are brought out for interment. The rate of deaths has steadily increased from 37.4 per thousand during the month of march last to 62.7 per thousand in July...

Lieutenant Colonel Chandler's report also pointed out deficiencies in the camp's guards, transportation system, and the accounting system of prisoners funds. It concluded with the recommendation that no more prisoners be sent to Andersonville and all the excess over 15,000 be removed to another camp site.

Colonel Chilton, Assistant Adjutant and Inspector General concurred with Colonel Chandler's recommendations and forwarded his report to the War Department with the comment, *"The condition of the prison at Andersonville is a reproach to us as a nation."*

Appendix 3

List of Prisoners of War from Pennsylvania Regiments Who died in Andersonville, Georgia

GRAVE	NAME	UNIT	COMPANY	DIED		GRAVE	NAME	UNIT	COMPANY	DIED
224	Attwood, Abr'm	C 18	I	Mar 29		4056	Anderson, J.	79	I	July 27
320	Armidster, M.	Cav4	A	Mar 30		4148	Aches, T.J.	7	H	July 28
408	Ackerman, C.	8	B	Apr 9		4149	Alcorn, Geo.W.	145	F	July 28
758	Arb, Simon	Cav4	C	Apr 27		4495	Archart, H.	51	C	July 29
846	Ailbeck, G.B.	52	F	May 3		4673	Allen, C.	Cav8	K	Aug 4
975	Algert, H.R.	54	F	May 9		4973	Andertin, J.	Cav 4	L	Aug 7
1282	Arble, Thos.	Cav13	A	May 26		5286	Aler, B.	101	D	Aug 11
1837	Alt, M.	21	K	June 11		5511	Ault, J.L.	101	C	Aug 13
2348	*Aikers, Geo.*	*90*	*H*	*June 23*		5862	Armstrong, C.	Cav4	C	Aug 16
2398	Alison, E.	55	K	June 24		6029	Anersen, John	91	C	Aug 18
2547	Anderson, D.	103	K	June 27		7163	Arnold, Dan	184	C	Aug 20
2648	Able, J.	54	F	June 28		7887	Angstedt, Geo W.	1	F	Sept 6
2956	Amagart, Eli	103	F	July 6		8185	Allen, J.L.	101	I	Sept 9
3018	Ackley, G.B.	Art3	B	July 7		8232	Ambler, C.	Cav13	D	Sept 9
3917	Alexander, M.	Cav1	F	July 14		8388	Alexander, W.	Res2	O	Sept 10
3967	Ardray, J.F.	13	F	July 25		8653	Armstrong, A.	7	K	Sept 13

8655 Arnold, L	73	A	Sept	13
8765 Altimus, Wm.	7	E	Sept	14
1743 Ainley, Wm.	Cav3	E	June	8
9150 Alcorn, J.W.	18	D	Sept	18
9896 Allison, D.B.	55	K	Sept	27
10487 Anderson, A.	133	F	Oct	7
10570 Allen, D.	126	A	Oct	9
10823 Allin, S.	Cav7	H	Oct	13
11419 Applebay, T.M.	149	K	Oct	24
11607 Antill, J.	61	I	Oct	28
11710 Auger, W.	118		Nov	1
11852 Affleck, T.	2	F	Nov	1
11860 Amandt, J.	184	D	Nov	6
12530 Atchinson, W.P	142	F	Jan25/65
228 Bull, Frank	Cav4	H	Mar24/64
249 Burton,Lafayette	18	D	Mar	30
332 Briggs, Andrew	13	H	Apr	7
427 Begler, A.	27	C	Apr	3
543 Breel, Jacob	27	H	Apr	14
569 Black, JamesCav	14	D	Apr	15
661 Bradley,Alex Cav	3	F	Apr	21
671 Burns, Sam	73	K	Apr	22
673 Barra, J.	54	F	Apr	22
822 Bayne, Wm.	145	I	May	1
874 Bradley, M.	Art3	A	May	4
897 Brown, Henry	*90*	*H*	*May*	*5*
938 Brown, D.	4	C	May	7
974 Batting,IsaacCav	8	H	May	9
1046 Baker, J.D.	57	F	May	12
1188 Butler, Wm.	*90*	*B*	*May*	*15*
1300 Boyd, Thomas	9	D	May	23
1309 Bryson, J.	Cav2	D	May	23
1327 Brining, J.	Cav13	B	May	24

1375 Burney, J.	Cav13	G	May	26
1393 Brown, J.B.	Cav4	K	May	26
1576 Bowman, Sam	Art3	B	June	3
1601 Berfert, R.	103	B	June	4
1654 Brumley, Geo.	Cav4	I	June	5
1790 Butler, J.D.	76	B	June	10
1859 Berkhawn, H.	73	G	June	12
1872 Brooks, D.S.	79		June	12
1923 Brian, Chas.	183	F	June	14
1999 Bixter, R.	73	C	June	15
2026 Burns, Owen	Cav13	C	June	15
2046 Bigler, M.	Cav4		June	15
2127 Brown, C.	Cav3	B	June	17
2134 Buckhannan,w.	Art3	B	June	18
2180 Ball, L.	26	K	June	19
2236 Barr, J.T.	Cav4	K	June	20
2323 Baker, Henry	Cav18	I	June	22
2483 Bisel, John	Cav18	K	June	25
2539 Balsley, Wm.	Cav20	F	June	26
2610 Brown, M.	Cav14	C	June	28
2727 Breun, J.	73	K	July	1
2733 Bolt, J.H.	Cav18	E	July	1
2741 Beam, John	76	E	July	1
2816 Burns, John	Cav13	A	July	3
2913 Bish, J.	108	F	July	5
2918 Belford, John	115	F	July	5
3005 Bryan, P.	Art5	A	July	7
3019 Barr, S.	103	G	July	7
3027 Braney, J	48	E	July	7
3051 Barnes, W.	101	H	July	8
3097 Butler, L.J.	118	E	July	10
3109 Brunt, A	110	G	July	10
3216 Bernine, A.A.	101	B	July	12

3294 Burns, James	103 F July 14	5948 Bohnaberger, A.	115 G Aug 17
3442 Brinton, J.	157 D July 17	5969 Boyer, F.	43 K Aug 17
3477 Baker, Wm.	103 F July 17	6061 Baker, James	101 C Aug 18
3535 Burnside, J.	57 H July 18	6074 Bower, G.W.	103 K Aug 18
3600 Black, W.O.	103 G July 19	6099 Bally, J.F.	18 D Aug 18
3693 Billing, J.L. Cav3 H July 21		6127 Benhand, J.A.	103 D Aug 19
3716 Brenlinger, W.R. 4 D July 21		6229 Bear, Samuel	55 G Aug 20
3808 Butler, C.P.	148 A July 22	6244 Boles, M.S.	Cav4 K Aug 20
3821 Batchell, D.	55 D July 23	6279 Bower, C.	101 C Aug 20
3917 Bright, E.	*90 I July 23*	6319 Birney, J.	Cav4 C Aug 20
3988 Bradford, L.	10 I July 26	6359 Bennett, A.	67 K Aug 21
4002 Berkley, M.	50 I July 26	6542 Blackman, W.	18 D Aug 23
4084 Backner, Adam	116 G July 27	6551 Bannon, P.	7 A Aug 23
4330 Barrett, J.	6 K July 30	6554 Baldwin, C.H. Cav2 K Aug 23	
4360 Brown, J.	53 G July 31	6604 Bennet, E.T.	149 I Aug 23
4402 Butler, D.	53 G July 31	6621 Bell, Thomas	11 E Aug 23
4494 Barton, James Cav4 B Aug 1		6660 Blair, John G.	46 F Aug 24
4500 Burke, J.	*90 A Aug 1*	6663 Breckinridge, W. 73 K Aug 24	
4610 Baker, E.	4 K Aug 3	6688 Bowman, A.	63 B Aug 24
4667 Behreas, A.	7 E Aug 4	6701 Boyd, J.W.	101 C Aug 24
4752 Bennet, Geo.	55 D Aug 5	6704 Bemer, Wm.	145 K Aug 24
4989 Bowers, J.	Art2 I Aug 7	6887 Brown, T.	Cav11 I Aug 26
5040 Bammratta,	73 D Aug 8	6928 Bryan, L.	106 F Aug 26
5071 Barber, C.	6 D Aug 8	7125 Bridaham, H.W.	55 H Aug 28
5084 Buck, B.F.	Cav2 K Aug 8	7181 Bemer, S.	184 E Aug 29
5113 Brown, M.	50 D Aug 9	7347 Ball, P.	49 H Aug 31
5324 Burlingame, A. 141 K Aug 9		7460 Barnes, W.	119 G Sept 1
5391 Bear, John	79 D Aug 12	7477 Bennett, J.	55 D Sept 1
5416 Bruce, John	10 C Aug 12	7541 Barnett, M.	145 K Sept 2
5526 Bower, Benj. Cav6 L Aug 13		7684 Black, J	143 I Sept 3
5587 Burnham, H.	143 F Aug 14	7747 Blair, J.G.	49 E Sept 3
5592 Broadbuck,A. Cav11 A Aug 14		7775 Brink, F.	Cav11 M Sept 4
5877 Browning, Thos.103 A Aug 16		7940 Browers, J.A.	184 F Sept 5

7963	Brumley, Fred.		54	K	Sept	6		
8072	Bright, Adam		101	K	Sept	7		
8073	Boland,		183	I	Sept	7		
8256	Barr, P.		103	C	Sept	9		
8286	Brown, L.		Cav8	C	Sept	9		
8356	Brown, A.		101	H	Sept	10		
8358	Brickenstaff, W.	101		I	Sept	10		
8363	Bruce, J.B.		101	F	Sept	10		
8413	Blosser, Jonas		Res7	H	Sept	11		
8434	Bowsteak, T.D.		106	H	Sept	11		
8499	Bicklet, E.H.		57	K	Sept	11		
8606	Boots, E.N.		101	H	Sept	12		
8719	Beattie, Robert		95	D	Sept	14		
8769	Boyer, J.M.		Cav7	F	Sept	14		
8795	Bentley, T.		54	H	Sept	14		
8794	Brown, P.		55	A	Sept	15		
8902	Baker, J.		184	C	Sept	16		
8917	Baker, Wm.		Cav11		Sept	16		
9147	Blake, E.		69	K	Sept	18		
9520	Boyler, James		7	E	Sept	22		
9632	Baldwin, A.		51	K	Sept	24		
9745	Bowers, F.		Cav5	A	Sept	25		
9809	Bonewell, W.W.		Cav14	C	Sept	26		
9952	Blair, George		Art7		Sept	28		
10201	Burdge, H.		Cav3	D	Oct	2		
10226	Byers, J.		22	E	Oct	2		
10260	Burns, J.		103	E	Oct	3		
10292	Brown, G.M.		10	I	Oct	4		
10357	Burgess, H.		27	C	Oct	5		
10534	Buck, D.C.		Cav2	L	Oct	8		
10577	Ballinger, George	87		D	Oct	9		
10674	Blackman, W.		84	A	Oct	11		
10758	Beightel, J.F.		51	G	Oct	12		
10779	Boice, J.N.		145	G	Oct	12		
10783	Bowling, J.		3	A	Oct	12		
10943	Barthart, I.		116	H	Oct	14		
10980	Baney, George		4	I	Oct	15		
10983	Bowyer, J.S.		55	E	Oct	15		
11024	Bunker, F.		55	K	Oct	16		
11087	Bowman, G.		149	E	Oct	18		
11322	Bissel, B.		142	F	Oct	22		
11329	Bruce, A.		11	I	Oct	23		
11434	Berk, G.		51	A	Oct	24		
11445	Ball, J		19	K	Oct	25		
14504	Bain, G.		183	G	Oct	26		
11528	Baney, I.		Cav4	I	Oct	26		
11556	Baker, B.H.		148	B	Oct	27		
11563	Brock, C.		46	A	Oct	27		
11569	Beighley, W.		103	C	Oct	27		
11597	Blair, John		106	H	Oct	28		
11611	Boyer, T.		11	F	Oct	28		
11635	Burr, E.		145	K	Oct	28		
11674	Bolinger, G.		87	D	Oct	30		
11818	Bayley, H.		66	K	Nov	4		
11894	Burch, W.		Art2	F	Nov	7		
11920	Burke, J.D.		Cav22	D	Nov	9		
11972	Bupp, L.		149	G	Nov	12		
12039	Bailey, J.J.		Art2	F	Nov	16		
12059	Bongar, David		184	C	Nov	17		
12079	Bond, C.C.		20	K	Nov	18		
12096	Brady, N.		Cav5	M	Nov	19		
12168	Brubaker, B.P.		79	D	Nov	26		
12177	Braddock, T.		77	C	Nov	27		
12418	Barrens, J.		Cav5	G	Jan	9/65		
12812	Barnett, J.		6	D	Mar	25/65		
2917	Brim, James		56	I	July	5/64		

63

12665	Bennett, J.	184	E	Feb16/65	2849	Carron, James	Cav4	C	July	4
45	Carter, Wm.	139	H	Mar 14	2884	Calean, Samuel	103	K	July	4
97	Chase, Wm. B.	Cav15	C	Mar 22	2995	Coleman, J.	Cav18	K	July	7
156	Compsey, James	Cav14	H	Mar 25	3320	Chase, F.M.	72	G	July	14
355	Carman, F.H.	54	F	Apr 2	3362	Clark, N.	Cav8	D	July	15
445	Coyle, P.	45	A	Apr 9	3417	Caton, W.T.	49	D	July	16
466	Crouch, Levi	40	I	Apr 9	3430	Couch, Benj.	50	H	July	17
479	Croghan, John	Cav3	A	Apr 9	3948	Coyle, Ed	58	E	July	25
548	Case, Daniel	8	M	Apr 14	3993	Curtey, L.	10	I	July	26
734	Connor, Andrus	Cav4	L	Apr 25	4045	Carpenter, L	12	K	July	27
837	Cravener, S.P.	Cav14	K	May 1	4117	Cantrill, M	6	B	July	28
869	Curry, A	119	E	May 3	*4263*	*Conklin, N.*	*90*	*K*	*July*	*29*
1015	Campbell, Wm.	Cav8	E	May 10	4331	Chapman, J.	Art3	B	July	30
1099	Case, Silas	Cav2	L	May 14	4353	Crawford, M	Cav14	G	July	31
1138	Carmichael, G	Cav18	K	May 16	4357	Cox, James	103	G	July	31
1186	Crisholm, J.H.	150	H	May 18	4369	Claybaugh, G.W.	Art2	F	July	31
1206	Caldwell, S.A.	Cav14	E	May 19	4512	Crock, L.	45	A	Aug	1
1232	Coburg, M.C.	Cav6	L	May 20	4682	Croup, W.S.	103	L	Aug	4
1490	Coon, J.H.	Cav18	K	May 31	4729	Cochran, C.	103	I	Aug	4
1498	Campbell, H.B.	103	E	May 31	4903	Chew, John	18	F	Aug	6
1540	Clatter, F.	Cav18	C	May 31	5177	Cranes, E.	Cav4	M	Aug	9
1702	Calihan, Thos.	Cav14	H	June 7	5375	Campbell, James	3	F	Aug	11
1781	Cephas, L	145	I	June 8	5417	Cregg, J.G.	54	I	Aug	12
1829	Carter, Wm.	101	K	June 11	5423	Cumberland, T.	Cav14	B	Aug	12
1832	Calvert, R.R.	6	B	June 11	5484	Conahan, M.	115	B	Aug	13
1871	Coombs, John	Art3		June 12	5578	Carpenter, W.C.	145	G	Aug	14
1873	Cox, J.A.	Cav13		June 12	5584	Campbell, R.D.	11	E	Aug	14
2069	Cooper, T.	Cav18	K	June 16	5623	Cox, L.	Cav7	B	Aug	14
2349	Curry, R.	73	F	June 23	5828	Cummings, Benj.	3	A	Aug	16
2399	Coyle, H.	Cav8	F	June 24	5979	Conor, J.N.	184	C	Aug	17
2455	Crouse, E.	141	A	June 25	6237	Corbin, W.	49	C	Aug	20
2695	Copple, F	54	H	June 30	6269	Campbell, R.G.	11	C	Aug	20
2713	Chapman, J.	7	H	July 1	6320	Coon, George	2	F	Aug	21

6336	Cameron, Wm.	101	A	Aug	21	9554	Crum, C.	149	G	Sept	23
6395	Connelly, Wm.	55	C	Aug	21	9639	Cline, J.	118	A	Sept	24
6430	Conner, J.	6	D	Aug	22	9773	Coulter, G.	45	K	Sept	25
6502	Cline, J	3	H	Aug	22	9823	Cummings, R	65	K	Sept	27
6615	Crawford, J.	77	E	Aug	23	9886	Callahan, M	52	D	Sept	27
6645	Coleman, C.	19	E	Aug	23	9931	Conrad, W.	Cav14	M	Sept	28
6746	Conly, John	101	A	Aug	24	10104	Campbell Wm.	13	D	Sept	30
6913	*Craft, A.*	*90*	*G*	*Aug*	*26*	10120	Coats, L.R.	139	H	Oct	1
7045	Corbert, F.C.	Cav11	L	Aug	26	10274	Crawford, George	1	F	Oct	3
7095	Carr, J.	51	G	Aug	28	10276	Cantler, J.L.	13	A	Oct	3
7116	Cathcart, Robert	103	H	Aug	29	10283	Cromich, F.	7	H	Oct	4
7209	Crain, J.	Cav4	H	Aug	29	10386	Cornelius, Wm.	Cav7		Oct	5
7456	Craig, William	103	D	Sept	1	10399	Cullingford, P.	55	C	Oct	6
7463	Clay, Henry	184	A	Sept	1	10443	Clark, W.	Cav5	K	Oct	7
7617	Curry, S.	140	C	Sept	2	10462	Canby, G.C.	Cav2	E	Oct	7
7632	Carroll, A	Cav2	A	Sept	2	10497	Cpoerhewer, Wm.	1	D	Oct	8
7669	Campbell, G.T.	Art3	A	Sept	3	10541	Culberton, Louis	73	B	Oct	9
7696	Criser, M.	54	F	Sept	3	10842	Corbin, M.	184	D	Oct	13
8117	Crawford, J.A.	103	B	Sept	8	10847	Clark, G.	Cav1	H	Oct	13
8169	Cole, J.C.	118	K	Sept	8	11005	Coe, George W.	145	E	Oct	16
8260	Chapman, —	18	A	Sept	8	11025	Clark, J.	3	D	Oct	16
8512	Coyle, M.	79	B	Sept	12	11250	Clark, H.	184	F	Oct	21
8594	Cuiver, J.	69		Sept	12	11309	Clark, E.B.	101	B	Oct	22
8665	Clutler, L.	11	C	Sept	13	11370	Carrol, W.	145	B	Oct	23
8700	Cavender, J.L.	119	E	Sept	14	11436	Crawford, L.	184	R	Oct	24
8884	Cysey, A. Heavy	Art3		Sept	15	11438	Cole, H.O.	Cav2	L	Oct	24
9094	Coffman, Wm.	13	F	Sept	18	11477	Campbell, C.A.	Cav11	C	Oct	26
9134	Cramer, E	55	F	Sept	18	11565	Creagan, G.	Cav1	F	Oct	27
9141	Church, C.H.	45	B	Sept	18	11614	Crawford M.	14	K	Oct	28
9269	Clark, J.	101		Sept	19	11656	Coyle, H.	54	K	Oct	30
9396	Coats, S.R.	135	C	Sept	20	11659	Craney, Geo.	Cav20	L	Oct	30
9410	Combs, S.	1	H	Sept	21	11800	Cregger, W.H.	Cav5	G	Nov	4
9508	Colonay, J.	145	F	Sept	22	11815	Chacon, A.W.	106	B	Nov	4

11826	Colebaugh, W.		60	K	Nov	5	3985	Dougherty, J.	7 E July 26
11876	Crandall, L		145	I	Nov	6	4087	Deron, Robert	149 B July 29
11922	Cleaveland, E	Cav10		I	Nov	8	4202	Drenkle, J.A.	79 K July 29
11993	Crampton, A.B.		143	B	Nov	13	5232	Dechmam, John	184 G July 29
12120	Cullen, T.I.		31	I	Nov	22	4481	Dodrick, Louis	50 I Aug 1
12141	Conway, C.C.	Art2		A	Nov	23	4491	Denton, M.	Cav9 B Aug 1
12255	Crompton, F.G.		71	F	Dec	10	4497	Day, William	97 A Aug 1
12295	Cone, S.		115	E	Dec	16	4625	Davis, J.	101 E Aug 3
12301	Culp, P.K.		138	B	Dec	17	4711	Dort, C.R.	Cav4 H Aug 4
12368	Connor, S.		112	H	Jan	1/65	4786	Dondle, Robert	101 A Aug 5
12424	Clark, J.		80	D	Jan	9	4792	Davy, H.	68 K Aug 5
12487	Collins, G.		118	E	Jan	19	4806	Davenbrook, J.J.	101 G Aug 5
12599	Cassell, D		20	E	Feb	6	4885	Delaney, J.	101 A Aug 6
12672	Clark, F.D.		7	C	Feb	12	4897	Dunbar, John	Cav14 M Aug 6
12818	Copeland, B	Cav14		D	Mar	29	4910	Dean, J.	148 F Aug 6
1961	Culbertson, J.	Cav13		B	June	14	5023	Dawlin, —	110 D Aug 8
152	Davidson, John		57	I	Mar	25	5256	Ditzell, L.	73 I Aug 10
866	Dorr, Phineas		119	K	May	3	5431	Davidson, George	57 C Aug 12
1020	Doran, Mack		63	D	May	11	5468	Dougherty, —	101 I Aug 13
1161	Duntler, Henry		51	K	May	16	5664	Decker, J.	45 B Aug 14
1338	Dooner, M.		2	K	May	24	5740	Day, Andrew H.	Cav2 H Aug 15
1463	Davis Richard,	Cav3		L	May	29	5746	Doran, P.	99 I Aug 15
1541	Deamott, J.K.		45	C	June	1	6017	Deal, F.	63 A Aug 17
1545	Davis, Isaac	Cav8		H	June	1	6045	Degroot, H.	Cav13 A Aug 18
2630	Dun, R.B.		101	B	June	29	6176	Defree, James	15 G Aug 19
2657	Donavan, J.		139	K	June	29	6226	Dodd, J.	18 F Aug 20
2716	Deily, Wm.		53	H	July	1	6316	Davis, William	153 A Aug 20
2938	Davis, M.	Cav22		B	July	6	6568	Dawney, George	148 B Aug 23
3338	Degret, M.	Cav15		M	July	15	9679	*Donavan, D.*	*90 B Aug 24*
3363	Davidson, Chas.		100	M	July	15	6678	Dunn, Johnes	69 F Aug 25
3741	Dallin, James	Cav8		H	July	21	6797	Dailey, M.	7 I Aug 25
3795	Davis, J.		103	A	July	22	6879	Dunn, John	184 A Aug 26
3873	Davis, M.H.		103	E	July	24	7053	Dakenfelt, J.	55 D Aug 28

7077	Deets, R.		3	A	Aug	28			
7282	Day, S.		13	A	Aug	30			
7360	Dively, J.		110	C	Aug	31			
7488	Dilks, C.		1	K	Sept	1			
7651	Dewell, Samuel		50	G	Sept	3			
7828	Dougherty, J		184	D	Sept	4			
8211	Dixon, J.		105	B	Sept	8			
8334	Dougherty, J.		73	F	Sept	10			
8569	Duff, J.		Cav4	B	Sept	12			
8579	*Dougherty, F.*		*90*	*C*	*Sept*	*12*			
8718	Durharse, B.		Cav11	G	Sept	14			
8828	Donnelly, J.		97	H	Sept	15			
8887	Dean, R.		Cav2	M	Sept	15			
9109	*Davidson, C.*		*90*	*G*	*Sept*	*18*			
9146	Driscoll, N.C.		26	I	Sept	18			
9191	Duffie, J		52	F	Sept	18			
9289	Delaney, E.		7	G	Sept	19			
10004	Davidson, G		12	K	Sept	29			
10193	Dougherty, M.		Cav3	D	Oct	2			
10436	Durkale, John		Cav1	F	Oct	6			
10917	Dalzell, J.G.		139	I	Oct	14			
11295	Derry, Fred.		20	C	Oct	22			
11350	Dichell, Espy		55	D	Oct	23			
11394	Dewitt, M.		Cav1	E	Oct	24			
11628	Davidson, S.		184	A	Oct	28			
11988	Dickens, Chas.		Art2	A	Oct	13			
12136	Dalrysuffle, J.E.		145	K	Oct	23			
12399	Donley, P.		120	G	Jan 5/65				
12575	Deeds, J.		Cav13	H	Feb	2			
11181	Dixon, B.		145	K	Oct 19/64				
972	Ellers, Henry		Cav13	H	May	9			
1081	Eisley, John		Cav18	K	May	14			
1436	Engle, Peter		Cav14	K	May	28			

2105	Elliott, John	Cav13	F	June	17
2794	Elliott, J.		69	D	July	2
3038	Erwin, C.		78	D	July	8
3052	Epsey, James		145	H	July	9
3295	Elliott, J.P.		103	D	July	14
3823	Ebright, Benj.	Cav9	A	July	23
4278	Eaton, Nat	Rifle1	E	July	30
4761	Ellenberger, P.	145	D	Aug	5
5687	Ennies, Andrew	145	K	Aug	15
6424	Ewetts, James	103	G	Aug	22
6607	Ellis, F.		53	G	Aug	23
6872	Eckles, E.		77	E	Aug	26
6889	Ensley, C.		184	A	Aug	26
7300	Ellis, H.H.	Cav18	I	Aug	30
7657	Egan, John		55	C	Sept	3
8066	Exline, Jacob		55	K	Sept	7
8543	Eichnor, C.		143	F	Sept	12
8964	Earlman, J.		7	K	Sept	16
10009	Elfrey, B.S.		7	K	Sept	29
10694	Elliott, John H.	83	D	Oct	11
10731	Erdibach, C.	Cav5	B	Oct	11
10799	Ervingfelts, J.	187	D	Oct	12
11834	Edgar, W.H.		7	G	Nov	5
11838	Erebefier, J.		5	B	Nov	5
12001	Etters, D.		145	D	Nov	14
12673	Ebhart, J.		87	E	Feb 18/65
9490	English, J.C.		100	K	Sept21/64
200	Fluher, John		73	D	Mar	28
511	Fich, John		83	B	Apr	12
791	Fry, L.		Cav4	D	Apr	28
1010	Fuller, H.		Cav13	H	May	10
1098	Fifer, Charles		27	I	May	14
1431	Fry, Alewx		Cav4	B	May	28

1728	Fink Peter	73	C	June 8
1957	Freeman, W.M.	Art 4	A	June 14
2078	Fulton, Thos.A.	103	H	June 17
2099	Friday, S.D.	101	H	June 17
2147	Fish, Chas. W.	101	B	June 18
2155	Farley, James	54	F	June 18
2261	Fox, George	78	E	June 21
2477	Flay, L.	26	G	june 25
2530	Funkhanna, Jas.	101	C	June 26
2537	Fatleam, A	50	D	June 26
2594	*Fargartus, T.*	*90*	*K*	*June 28*
2853	Fancy, George	Cav13	F	July 4
3088	Ford, M.	53	K	July 19
3258	Fisher, B.M.	101	H	July 13
3582	French, A.	Art2	G	July 19
3742	Forsyth, J.	Cav18	H	July 21
2870	Fingley, John	Cav14	D	July 24
4307	Flick, L.	184	G	July 30
4439	Filey, J.H.	53	E	July 31
4452	Foreman, G.S.	Cav1	B	Aug 1
4521	Flashorse, B	Cav12	A	Aug 2
4586	Flynn, M	Cav13	B	Aug 2
4642	Fewer, E.	87	H	Aug 3
4668	File, C.	145	D	Aug 4
5062	Fish, J.	85		Aug 8
5172	Fleming, W.	97	E	Aug 9
5586	Flickinger, John	50	B	Aug 14
5788	Ferry, W.	79	A	Aug 15
5873	Fee, George M.	103	G	Aug 16
6092	Faiss, A.	145	E	Aug 18
6134	Farman, E.	57	E	Aug 19
6155	Feltharsen, —	145	G	Aug 19
6180	Fatlenger, F.	53	K	Aug 19

6365	Fanen, J.F	Reserve7	G	Aug 21
6396	Finlaugh, S.	Cav14	G	Aug 21
6649	Fox, R.	155	H	Aug 23
6675	Fritzman, J.W.	18	K	Aug 24
6694	Finlin, Thomas	143	G	Aug 24
6881	Fuller, G.	Cav2	A	Aug 26
6884	Frederick, L.	148	B	Aug 26
6890	French, James	101	H	Aug 26
6892	Ford, Thomas	7	I	Aug 26
7041	Fullerton, E.	99	E	Aug 27
7097	Fester, John	103	B	Aug 28
7169	Fisher, W.	54	I	Aug 29
7198	Fry, —	101	E	Aug 29
7575	Fitzgerald, M.	145	K	Sept 2
7588	Fahy, John	Cav13	B	Sept 2
7776	Fritz, D.	Cav18	K	Sept 4
8006	Felter, H.M.	Cav13	K	Sept 6
8149	Fullerton, J.	118	I	Sept 8
8175	Fetterman, J.	48	H	Sept 8
8321	Francis, N.	69	G	Sept 10
8631	Fagan, P.	118	F	Sept 13
9062	Fisher, C.	Cav4		Sept 17
9099	Floyd, B.	67	K	Sept 18
9232	Farr, J.C.	107	H	Sept 19
9869	Faith, Alex	183	C	Sept 27
10176	Fessenden, N.E.	149	F	Oct 1
10408	Fingley, S.	14	B	Oct 6
10639	Fisher, W.	101	E	Oct 10
10667	Flynn, S.	76	C	Oct 11
10688	Free, J.	145	H	Oct 11
11026	Flemming, J	97	E	Oct 16
11112	Flanney, J.	106	K	Oct 18
11164	Ferguson, J.R	Cav11	D	Oct 19

11367	Fox, M.	Cav8	H	Oct	23
11378	Frill, D	55	C	Oct	24
11601	Ferguson, John	134	A	Oct	28
11802	Fisher, Henry	115	E	Nov	4
11916	Freed, S.	53	B	Nov	8
11962	Fairbanks, E.	140	A	Nov	11
12000	Fagley, C.	Cav14	I	Nov	14
12025	Forest, S.L.	149	I	Nov	15
12207	Foster, C.W.	76	B	Dec	1
12244	Falkenstine, F.	148	C	Dec	8
12336	Fruce, J.	52	A	Dec	26
12445	Fisk, J.	67	H	Jan	13/65
12605	Faile, W.D.	Cav20	A	Feb	7/65
71	Goodman, Robert	Cav13	M	Mar	19/64
131	Gesse, Christian	54	F	Mar	23
314	Graffell, Wm.	73	B	Apr	2
529	Guley, J.	145	G	Apr	12
573	Green, Wm.	Cav3	A	Apr	16
968	Garman, B.	Cav18	E	Apr	9
1001	Greer, J.A.	Cav3	E	May	10
1008	Graham, W.J.	4	C	May	10
1063	Goodman, Henry	27	I	May	13
1302	Gray, M.	7	B	May	23
1373	Gilbert, John	29	G	May	25
1399	Gilroy, Berney	73	F	May	26
1528	Getts, B.	84	G	May	31
1649	Griffil, G.W.	Cav13	L	June	5
1761	Geest, J.W.	57	I	June	9
1793	Gardner, —Negro	8	F	June	10
1930	Geusle, John	Cav19	F	June	13
1939	Goerlt, E.	73	H	June	14
2060	Galliger, F	Cav13	B	June	16
2084	Gillmore, James	110	E	June	17
2297	Gunn, Alex	Cav4	D	June	21
2356	Greenwald, G.	27	H	June	23
2531	Gumbert, A.	103	B	June	26
2587	Gettings, J.	Rifle1	C	June	28
2944	Gross, Samuel	51	E	July	6
2955	Gotwalt, H.	55	D	July	6
2988	Griffin, J.	103	I	July	7
2992	George, A.	149	G	July	7
2996	Gists, H.	103	H	July	7
3037	Gilleland,Wm.	Cav14	B	July	8
3528	Gorsuch, M.A.	110	B	July	18
3509	Gibbs, E.	Cav18	K	July	19
4944	Gost, W.H.	Cav5	K	Aug	7
5422	Gregg, T.	139	K	Aug	12
5655	Gross, John	62	K	Aug	14
5735	Gregg, D.	142	A	Aug	15
5737	Graham, Wm.	103	F	Aug	15
5803	Graham, D.	Cav4	K	Aug	16
5881	Grouse, G.	145	C	Aug	16
5888	Gettenher, D.M.	103	I	Aug	16
6006	Geand, C.	Cav4	M	Aug	17
5288	Gladen, A.	21	C	Aug	11
6140	Garrett, James	51	K	Aug	19
6158	Gunn, J.W.	101	H	Aug	19
6384	Gamble, O.J.	77	A	Aug	21
6389	Gallagher, S.	48	A	Aug	21
6897	Green, J.C.	Cav13	D	Aug	26
7223	Gibson, D	56	A	Aug	29
7320	Graham, J.	56	B	Aug	30
7340	Geary, D.	184	G	Aug	30
7357	Groves, A.T.	45	A	Aug	31
7352	Glass, Wm.	55	C	Aug	31
7527	Griffith, A.	54	F	Sept	1

7589	Granger, E.H.	55	C	Sept 2
7679	Geslin, E.H.	4	G	Sept 3
7773	Giles, C.	7	K	Sept 4
7839	Gross, G.W.	79	A	Sept 4
8109	Galbraith, C	11	K	Sept 6
8311	Garrison, W.	8	K	Sept 10
8448	Gallagher, Wm.	Cav5	D	Sept 11
8735	Griffin, J.C.	Cav5	D	Sept 14
9005	Gearhan, S.	142	C	Sept 17
9210	Griffin, D.	11	E	Sept 19
9326	Gilbert, H.	53	F	Sept 20
9437	Gorbay, F.J.	Cav19	M	Sept 21
9503	Goodman, F.	55	H	Sept 21
9764	Grubbs, J	103	F	Sept 25
9776	Gibson, J.	11	D	Sept 26
9792	Glenn, Wm.	101	C	Sept 26
9811	Grear, R.	73	H	Sept 26
9966	Gilbert, D.	138	B	Sept 28
9989	Garrett, F.	139	G	Sept 29
10051	Gibson, D.G.	Cav16	A	Sept 30
10127	Gemperling, Wm.	79	A	Oct 1
10468	Grant, M.	Cav18	I	Oct 7
10615	Griffin, J.	56	A	Oct 10
10706	Gimberling, I.	184	F	Oct 11
11060	Greathouse, E.	14	B	Oct 17
11197	Grabb, M.P.	83	H	Oct 20
11299	Gilbert, A.F.	Cav14	F	Oct 20
11496	Grant, J	6	E	Oct 26
11573	Ganse, R.	22	B	Oct 27
11806	Gordon, R.	65	F	Nov 4
11901	green, W.S.	12	I	Nov 7
12181	Giher, P.	73	H	Nov 27
12237	George, F.	Cav18	D	Dec 6

12337	Garrety, Thomas	106	C	Jan2/65
12411	Gates, J.	Cav11	E	Jan 65
12432	Grunnel, John	26	H	Jan11/65
5843	Gillespie, J.	11	A	Aug16/64
5118	Gibbons, Wm.	11	H	Aug 9
6228	Gallagher, T.	101	A	Aug 21
5971	Gray, L.	163	D	Aug 17
423	Hanson, T.R.	119	E	Apr 7
470	Herbert, Otto	73	A	Apr 9
555	Hoffmaster, L.	16	H	Apr 14
654	Hamilton, J.G.	Cav4	L	Apr 20
711	Hall, J. Negro	8	E	Apr 24
769	Hessimer, P.	73	E	Apr 27
988	Hammons, J.	Art3	A	May 10
990	Heager, J.	2	B	May 10
1080	Huff, Arthur	54	F	May 14
1113	Hates, Charles	2	H	May 15
1225	Henderson, R.	Cav18	D	May 20
1311	Heckley, M.	Cav4	M	May 23
1420	Hill, H.C.	18	K	May 28
1483	Holtenstein, G.W.C.	18	I	May 30
1562	Henen, Pat	145	E	June 2
1650	Hendricks, N.	Cav4	D	June 5
1768	Holmes, Robt.	Cav12	H	June 9
2011	Hannah, Thomas	Cav4	D	June 15
2153	Hammer, P.C.	Cav18	D	June 18
2189	Harts, John	51	H	June 19
2387	Hooks, T.	103	D	June 24
2450	Hiler H.	50	C	June 25
2551	Hammer, John	73	G	June 27
2707	Howard, James	83	I	June 30
2723	Henderson, A	58	F	JUly 1
2786	Hollibaugh, W.	57	C	July 2

2800	Hastings, J.	118	D	July 2
2916	Homer, D.	Cav13	F	July 5
3020	Holley, E.F.	57	A	July 7
3201	Harrington, John	55	C	July 12
2	Headley, J.D.	18	G	Mar 15/64
3379	Height, S.C.	55	H	July 16
3439	Hughes, John	118	A	July 17
3525	Heenan, John	Cav14	F	July 18
3554	Hazlet, J.	Cav4	G	July 18
3663	Hester, I.P.	7	H	July 18
3626	Heth, R	2	A	July 20
3785	Harrington, J.W.	Cav3	A	July 22
3792	Haller, Peter	139	K	July 22
3836	Harvey, P.D.	57	B	July 23
3853	Hollenbeck, J.A.	55	B	July 24
3929	Hall,, Henry	53	H	July 25
3953	Haller, A.	73	A	July 25
4105	Hartlick, C.	99	E	July 27
4136	Hiffefinger, V.	14	K	July 28
4147	Hobbs, A.	141	H	July 28
4154	Hill, P.	101	B	July 28
4222	Hoover, John	Cav18	E	July 29
4332	Holland, J.	143	I	July 31
4370	Hilt, John	73	I	July 31
4379	Hardinger, W.	147	B	July 31
4431	Hill, Thomas	18	L	July 31
4474	Hans, John	116	J	Aug 1
4790	Haffinger, J.	91	C	Aug 5
4921	Hick, G	12	B	Aug 6
5045	Haher, C.	Cav14	B	Aug 8
5080	Hall, —	149	I	Aug 8
5082	Hunter, L.	63	C	Aug 8
5131	Hardis, J.L.	11	A	Aug 9
5178	Harden, M.	Res.Home Grd	F	Aug 9
5281	Huffman, Chas.	Cav7	K	Aug 11
5284	Hickey, D.C.	Cav3	C	Aug 11
5289	Hanson, J.	76	B	Aug 11
5486	Harder, —	184	C	Aug 13
5575	Hoffmaster, G.	20	F	Aug 14
5688	Heinback, S.	116	H	Aug 15
5694	Holinbeck, D.	101	E	Aug 17
6175	Honigan, C.	55	C	Aug 19
6302	Henry, R.W.	4	H	Aug 20
6367	Hill, J.E.	Cav2	L	Aug 21
6481	Hollingsworth,J.	Neg.8A		Aug 22
6597	Hoffmaster, L.	73	I	Aug 23
6635	Hazenffiucey,J.	Bat26		Aug 23
6711	Hoch, John	103	K	Aug 24
6752	Haden, R.	119	A	Aug 24
6792	Hogan, Thomas	103	K	Aug 25
6845	Hurling, A.	57	C	Aug 25
6910	Hammer, John	Art3	B	Aug 26
7000	Hoy, J.	101	F	Aug 27
7102	Houseman, G.	118	I	Aug 28
7286	Holloman, Wm.	102	G	Aug 30
7328	Hopes, W.	Art2	A	Aug 30
7422	Havert, B.	53	I	Aug 31
7491	Hallinger, C.	63	D	Sept 1
7531	Hill, E.	110		Sept 1
7537	Henry, A.B.	103	E	Sept 1
7568	Hobson, B.F.	7	G	Sept 2
7571	Harman, John	14	H	Sept 2
7588	Harris, A.	Cav2	K	Sept 2
7613	Homiker, J.	119	H	Sept 2
7661	Hockenbroch, J.	Art2	F	Sept 3
7661	Hughes, J.	Cav11	B	Sept 3

No.	Name	Regt	Co.	Date
7682	Hoover, S.P.	7	H	Sept 3
7687	Hunter, Charles	3	A	Sept 3
7881	Holmes, S.	140	B	Sept 5
7965	Hutton, James	118	I	Sept 6
7990	Hazel, George	Cav2	D	Sept 6
8254	Hecker, G.	Reserves6	C	Sept 9
8462	Henry, O.H.	Cav2	L	Sept 11
8566	Heselport, J.F.	68	G	Sept 12
8582	Hopkins, —	50	K	Sept 12
9088	*Hensey, —*	*90*	*C*	*Sept 18*
9118	Hooker, Wm.	8	G	Sept 18
9123	Holdhaus, C.	63	E	Sept 18
9404	Houghbough, J.	143	D	Sept 21
9434	Hanks, J.	1	A	Sept 21
9433	hartzel, J.	7	I	Sept 21
9532	Houston, D.	4	B	Sept 22
9579	Harmony, J.	169	H	Sept 23
9843	Heninshalt, W.	149	E	Sept 27
9884	Hibbane, J.	99	H	Sept 27
9904	Hughly, John	69	D	Sept 27
10022	Hamilton, B.	183		Sept 29
10070	Holden, Isaac	7	G	Sept 30
10109	Harper, R.	103	B	Sept 30
10239	Hicks, J.F.	Cav14	A	Oct 2
10349	Hammond, J.	10	D	Oct 5
10385	Hill, S.M.	14	D	Oct 5
10430	Haldwell, P.	Cav7	E	Oct 6
10448	Hiller, S.	64	D	Oct 7
10474	Howe, M.A.	Cav12	B	Oct 7
10538	Hand, H	58		Oct 8
10571	Holden, P.	Cav12	B	Oct 9
10574	Hayes, J.	Cav15	G	Oct 9
10640	Hands, J.	106	A	Oct 10
10670	Hull, Ed	77	G	Oct 11
10804	Hennessey, P.	49	H	Oct 12
10814	Hunbach, J.	116	G	Oct 12
10862	Hoberg, A.J.	Cav2	M	Oct 13
10903	Hannesay, A.	55	I	Oct 14
10906	Hall, A.	118	E	Oct 14
10952	Hoover, S.	79	G	Oct 14
10962	Huffman, S.	64	C	Oct 15
11033	Happy, G.	101	K	Oct 16
11092	Harty, James	148	I	Oct 18
11113	Horton, S.	106	I	Oct 18
11183	Hess, G.	118	D	Oct 19
11194	Hepsey, M.	73	K	Oct 20
11383	Hunter, J.	Cav5	M	Oct 24
11481	Hart, J.	7	I	Oct 26
11219	Hunter, J.	Cav14	M	Oct 20
11495	Hardinwick, J.	2	C	Oct 26
11609	Hosaflock, H.A.	Cav6	E	Oct 28
11643	Hackett, J.	30	D	Oct 30
11702	*Hoover, J.*	*90*	*A*	*Oct 31*
11799	Hagerty, W.R.	7	G	Nov 4
11897	Hart, M.	11	K	Nov 7
12215	Hyatt, J.F.	118	F	Dec 3
12260	Healy, J.B.	100	M	Dec 11
12306	Hammond, QW.	20	K	Dec 18
12610	heneman, E.L.	5	C	Feb7/65
12632	Healey, J.	143	K	Feb10/65
12719	Hummell, J.	87	B	Mar 2/65
7020	Hazen, M.J.	101	H	Aug22/64
3474	Hall, B.	105	F	July 17
10227	Haman, I.	118	E	Oct 1
124	Isheart, N.	Cav18	G	Mar 23
1401	Illy, Tobias	27	G	Mar 27

10405	Irvin, T.	Cav15	M	Oct	8	8318 Johnson, J.	45 I Sept 10
10616	Ireton, S.R.	138	I	Oct	10	8853 Jolly, James	101 H Sept 15

10405 Irvin, T.　　Cav15 M Oct　8　　8318 Johnson, J.　　　45 I Sept 10
10616 Ireton, S.R.　　138 I Oct 10　　8853 Jolly, James　　101 H Sept 15
11560 Irwin, W.　　184 A Oct 27　　9303 Jones, P.　　　63 F Sept 20
831 Ingersoll, Sam　　3 D May 1　　9351 Jordan, J.M.　　149 D Sept 20
233 Johnson, John J.　45 I Mar 29　　9378 Jacobs, J.S.　Cav6 F Sept 20
463 *Johnson, Charles*　*90 C Apr 9*　　9982 Jeffries, C.　　4 B Sept 29
565 Johnson, John　Cav2 G Apr 15　　9999 Jones, T.　　101 B Sept 29
576 Jacobs, Jacob　Cav2 M Apr 9　　10735 Jabin, James　55 E Oct 11
1303 Jones, Wm.　　145 A May 23　　10987 Jones, A.　　27 D Oct 16
1595 Jones, J.　　147 C June 3　　11058 Johnson, Wm.　184 D Oct 17
1840 Jones, Wm.　　26 C June 11　　11430 Jordan, Thomas　148 Oct 24
2108 Jones, O.　　Cav4 D June 17　　11539 Jenks, J.C.　115 H Oct 27
2312 Johnson, Wm.　Art3 A June 22　　12007 Johnson, L.　118 C Nov 4
2593 Jones, R.　　103 D June 28　　12331 Jack, J.P.　　7 E Dec 24
2914 Jordan, D.W.　103 B July 5　　2889 Johnson, A.G.　103 I July 4
3409 Johnson, D.　45 I July 18　　2 Kelly, Charles II 71 H Mar 1
3510 Jennings, H.　45 G July 18　　238 Kelly, H.S.　Cav13 H Mar 30
3885 Jones, Wm.　55 C July 24　　266 Kuntzelman, J.　63 E Mar 31
4057 John, Thomas　54 E July 27　　1024 Kenny, Wm.　12 F May 11
4093 Jones, J.　　79 A July 27　　1824 Kyle, Wm.　　5 H June 10
4540 Johnson, J.W.　50 G Aug 2　　1875 Kelly, Peter　73 June 12
4590 Jameson, Wm.　103 H Aug 3　　2076 Knight, John　Cav7 K June 17
4817 Johns, Robert　101 I Aug 5　　2335 Kehoe, Moses　8 H June 22
5295 Johnson, H.　Art2 I Aug 11　　2639 Kenoan, M.A.　Cav14 L June 29
5516 Jacobs, B.G.　150 F Aug 13　　3048 King, C.　　6 C July 8
5871 Jones, Robert　100 A Aug 16　　3187 Klech, N.　　54 A July 12
6197 Jones, T.　　101 I Aug 19　　3265 Klink, A.　　101 C July 13
6200 Jones, W.E.　27 B Aug 19　　3471 Kemp, E.　　103 A July 17
6317 Jones, S　　49 G Aug 22　　3634 Keeston, E　103 I July 20
6760 Joslin, J.　145 I Aug 25　　4162 Kagman, J.T.　45 B July 28
6817 Jober, J.　　77 B Aug 25　　4293 Kuffman, S.D.　45 E July 30
6931 Jarmter, C.　7 A Aug 26　　4545 Kauf, J.　　Art2 B Aug 2
7566 Johnson, Charles 53 G Sept 2　　4895 Kelley, O.F.　148 B Aug 6

5058	Kock, H.		21	H	Aug	8	11322	King, J.R.	55	K Oct	23
5145	Kawell, John	Cav18	E	Aug	9	11384	Kelley, E.	Cav7	F Oct	24
5154	Keyes, Alex C.	Cav16	H	Aug	9	11463	King, R.	6	E Oct	26
5208	Kester, L.	149	F	Aug	10	11645	Kramer, George	116	G Oct	30
5443	Kelley, T.	Cav13	H	Aug	12	12695	Knox, J.	184	A Feb23/65
5851	Kahn, R	96	K	Aug	13	8676	Kerer, H.N.	63	EJuly20/64
5718	Keister, John M.	103	A	Aug	15	88	Liesen, Lewis	Cav13	A Mar	21
5744	Keeley, Wm.	Cav13	A	Aug	15	243	Lancaster, E.	Cav14	F Mar	30
6028	Kauffman, B.F.	45	K	Aug	18	297	Luck, W.	Cav11	H Apr	1
6084	Kemper, J.	73	D	Aug	18	549	Lynch, Adam	Cav6	L Apr	14
6459	Kiger, Wm.	Cav3	C	Aug	22	1403	Levy, Frank	Cav3	H May	27
6497	Kenter, A.W.	67	B	Aug	22	1429	Liesine, W.	13	E May	28
6514	Kniver, S.	184	F	Aug	22	1579	Lindine, J.	Art3	A June	3
6628	Krigle, H.	11	K	Aug	23	1588	Little, M.	106	F June	3
6965	Krader, W.O.	55	H	Aug	27	1621	Luhaus, Melter	145	A June	4
7005	King, M.	Cav3	A	Aug	27	2250	Lackey, James	183	D June	21
7372	Keller, A	9	M	Aug	31	2379	Leach, J.	Cav3	D June	23
7553	Keller, M.	103	G	Sept	1	3091	Larimer, J.	11	E July	9
7781	Kyle, Wm.	118	F	Sept	7	3734	Ladbeater, James	7	K July	21
8210	Kinsman, F.P.	184	F	Sept	8	3305	Link, P.	98	H July	14
8734	Kanford, John C.,	SMC5	Sept	14	3306	Long, A.	118	H July	14
8799	kaufman, J.	45	E	Sept	17	3869	Lanigan, N.	Cav13	L July	15
9139	Kipp, W.	Cav12	D	Sept	18	3404	Lewis, Ed	101	I July	16
9533	Kinmick, T.	145	K	Sept	23	3448	Leonard, George	49	G July	17
9630	Kearney, L.	50	F	Sept	24	3489	Logan, B.	90	B July	17
10335	Kerr, B.	149	B	Oct	4	3545	Lee, James	Cav13	L July	18
10367	Kirby, J.A.	101	E	Oct	5	4312	Long, D.F.B.	101	I July	30
10439	Kline, Ross	184	F	Oct	6	4434	Lambert, W.	Cav4	K July	31
10502	Kennedy, J.	152	A	Oct	8	4696	Larrison, W.	Cav14	C Aug	4
10698	King, M.	11	K	Oct	11	4818	Lewis, A.	Cav3	D Aug	5
10747	Kirkwood, H.	101	C	Oct	11	4857	Laughlin, J.	101	E Aug	6
10926	Knieper, C.	89	F	Oct	14	4907	Lahman, C.	73	C Aug	6
11238	Kurtz, J.	55	K	Oct	21	4929	Livingston, J.K.	2	B Aug	6

5199	Long, Augustus	55	H	Aug	10	11907	Ladd, A.	53	M	Nov	7
5225	Loudin, H.N.	14	H	Aug	10	12192	Lape, J.	18	K	Nov	28
5314	Lacock, Hugh	116	E	Aug	11	12210	Lewis, D.S.	53	K	Dec	2
6252	*Lodiss, H.*	*90*	*H*	*Aug*	*20*	12489	Linsey, D.	77	G	Jan19/65	
6636	Leach, James	49	E	Aug	23	5699	Ledwick, F.M.	139	C	Aug15/64	
6783	Light, S.	143	H	Aug	25	7084	Latchem, David	Cav4	K	Aug	28
7145	LaBelt, J.	21	F	Aug	29	7307	Lochery, A	Cav14	E	Aug	30
7938	Lemon, John E.	Cav4	I	Sept	6	5985	Logan, W.	97	A	Aug	17
7950	Lockhard, J.	145	H	Sept	8	6030	Loudon, S.	101	A	Aug	18
8405	Lepley, Charles	103	E	Sept	10	6058	Layton, Samuel	181	A	Aug	18
8754	Layman, F.	49	B	Sept	10	6071	Lamb, C.	71	B	Aug	18
8833	Laughlin, J.L.	1	H	Sept	15	6082	Lane, Amos	Cav6	E	Aug	18
8895	Lester, W.H.	Cav7	I	Sept	16	6152	Lehnich, John	Art2	F	Aug	19
8904	Lippoth, J.	5	E	Sept	16	753	Lenard, M.	Cav13	D	Apr	26
9085	Logne, S.	26	A	Sept	18	761	Lord, G.W.	141	E	Apr	27
9291	Leary, C.	83	K	Sept	19	871	Loudon, Samuel	2	F	May	4
9647	Loden, J.	Cav4	C	Sept	24	183	Maynard, John	105	G	Mar	27
10066	Laytin, P.	110	D	Sept	30	208	Missle, Val	47	C	Mar	28
10086	Lutz, P.M.	21	G	Sept	30	225	Miller, Daniel	Cav13	H	Mar	29
10091	Lebos, C.	116	D	Sept	30	361	Martin, J.F.	Cav14	K	Apr	2
10273	Limar, W.	140		Oct	3	461	McEntire, W.	51	F	Apr	9
10298	Long, W.	67	G	Oct	4	538	Mine, Josh	54	F	Apr	14
10372	Long, P.	Cav11	C	Oct	5	586	Marple, S.L.	14	A	Apr	17
10549	Lancaster, C	119	B	Oct	8	605	McKissick, John	23	F	Apr	18
10572	Lynch, W.J.	Cav3	I	Oct	9	667	Myers, G.	Cav1	E	Apr	22
10580	Labor, R.	7	F	Oct	10	736	McKeever, E.L.	71	F	Apr	25
10687	Luchford, R.	143	F	Oct	11	773	McDonald, R.	23	C	Apr	28
10873	Lang, I.	110	C	Oct	13	780	McCarthy, James	Cav18	E	Apr	28
11604	Leuchlier, J.	5		Oct	16	969	McQueeny, W.	79	B	May	9
11255	lantz, Wm.	17	C	Oct	21	1006	Meyer, John	Cav2	E	May	10
11465	Lewis, J.	Cav4	L	Oct	26	1128	McKey, J.	Cav1	I	May	15
11728	Luther, I.	Cav4	L	Nov	1	1139	McMahon, J.	73	F	May	16
11869	Lego, George	12	A	Nov	6	1147	McKnight, J.E.	57	B	May	16

1151	McHale,	Cav14	D	May	16	3065	Morris, Calvin	53	D July 9
1185	Moser, John	Cav13	B	May	18	3133	McCulaskey, J.E.	Cav4	K July 10
1273	McCollen, W.	Cav4	L	May	22	3151	Mattiser, B.	57	F July 11
1287	Milligan, J.	61	F	May	22	3172	Madden, Daniel	149	G July 11
1308	McCartney, M	73	B	May	23	3250	Myers, M.	103	E July 13
1460	Murray, John	Cav13	E	May	29	3374	Mink, H.	Art3	A July 16
1586	Miles, Lewis	Cav4	I	June 3		3467	Meaker, E.N.	155	H July 17
1643	Myers, J.R.	Cav13	M	June 5		3481	McKeon, John	101	H July 17
1722	Marshall, M.M.	78	E	June 8		3488	Mihan, J.	139	D July 17
1748	Moyer, YHomas	103	E	June 9		3939	Mahoney, John	Cav1	D July 20
1792	Miller, M.	118	A	June 10		3690	McCarron, J.	Cav4	A July 21
1858	Mellose, J.	Cav4	C	June 12		3766	Myers, John	116	D july 22
1907	Miller, Henry	8	G	June 13		3971	Martin, G.	45	I July 25
1982	Muchollans, J.	101	K	June 15		4016	McDermott, J.M.	70	F July 26
2056	Monny, W.H.	Cav3	A	June 16		4123	McGee, James	103	I July 28
2058	Mitchell, J.J.	101	K	June 16		4197	Moore, M.G.	Art1	A July 29
2159	Moran, J.	101	C	June 20		4241	Marquet, M.	6	M july 30
2265	McCutchen, J.	Cav4	C	June 21		4407	McKeever, John	100	A July 31
2278	Milton, Wm.	Cav19	H	June 21		4414	McFarland, James	55	E July 31
2333	Myers, F.	27	H	June 22		4546	Moan, james	101	K Aug 2
2364	Myers, Peter	76	G	June 23		4607	Martin, Bryant	7	F Aug 3
2388	Morton, T.	79	I	June 24		4635	McKeral, James	14	K Aug 3
2409	McCabe, J.	Cav3	L	June 24		4710	Mathews, C.W.	145	B Aug 4
2411	McKay, M.J.	103	B	June 24		4734	Moore, —	71	I Aug 4
2493	Murray, James	67	E	June 26		4796	McDevitt, J.	Art3	D Aug 5
2503	Martin, A.J.	Cav4	E	June 26		4824	Miller, H.	Cav14	I Aug 5
2508	Morris, J.	Cav18	A	June 26		4876	Mills, Wm.	150	G Aug 6
2653	McManus, —	77	B	June 29		4898	Muldanay, M.	96	K Aug 6
2684	Mipes, J.	101	B	June 30		5068	Martain, John	103	E Aug 8
2690	Morris, G.	77	G	June 30		5069	Measler, James	103	E Aug 8
2798	Marsh, D.	50	D	July 2		5139	McCaffrey, John	Art3	A Aug 9
2831	McCane, Charles	14	C	July 3		5159	Martin, C.	Cav8	A Aug 9
3017	McRath, J.	48	C	July 3		5266	Marey, H.F.	103	F Aug 10

5291 Mohr, J.R.	14	G	Aug	11
5415 McCarty, Dennis	101	K	Aug	12
5433 McGee, J.	14	H	Aug	12
5595 Mickelson, B.	Cav16	B	Aug	14
5642 McClough, L.C.	18	C	Aug	14
5704 Miller, John	101	G	Aug	15
5723 McCann, John	Art3	A	Aug	15
5809 Montgomery, R.	62	A	Aug	16
5868 McQuillen, A.	Art6	L	Aug	16
5893 McCuller, S.	Cav4	B	Aug	16
5926 Mulchey, J.A.	50	D	Aug	17
5988 Mann, James	119	G	Aug	17
6014 McPherson, D.	103	F	Aug	17
6038 Moore, C,	103	G	Aug	18
6148 McCracker, J.	53	K	Aug	19
6294 McLaughlin, Jas.	Cav4	A	Aug	20
6441 McWilliams, H.	92	I	Aug	21
6480 Martin, John	103	D	Aug	22
6532 McGan, J.	Cav18		Aug	23
6664 McKee, —	144	C	Aug	24
6689 Manner, M.	73	K	Aug	24
6910 McGlann, H.	143	B	Aug	26
6925 McGuigan, H.C.	7	K	Aug	26
7026 Marks, P.	143	B	Aug	27
7061 Moore, M.J.	107		Aug	28
7107 Moyer, William H.	55	K	Aug	28
7119 Miller, John L.	53	K	Aug	28
7127 McAfee, James	72	F	Aug	28
7175 Moore, Thomas	69	D	Aug	29
7263 Martin, John	77	C	Aug	30
7265 Musser, John	77	D	Aug	30
7305 Moser, S.	103	E	Aug	30
7333 Morris, John	183	G	Aug	3
7407 Marchin, William	50	E	Aug	31
7512 Millinger, John H.	7	C	Sept	1
7602 Moorhead, J.S.	103	D	Sept	2
7719 Myers, H.	9	A	Sept	3
7875 Mayer, W.	8	M	Sept	5
7925 Mays, N.J.	103	H	Sept	5
8027 Murphy, A.	Cav13	I	Sept	6
8047 McKnight, J.	Cav18	I	Sept	6
8122 Miller, J.	101	C	Sept	8
8123 Mullings, W.	145	G	Sept	8
8128 Munager, W	Cav13	L	Sept	8
8134 Mehaffey, J.M.	Cav16	B	Sept	8
8153 McCantley, W.	Art2	A	Sept	8
8158 McLane, T.	12	E	Sept	8
8194 McKink, J.	119	D	Sept	8
8216 Mansfield, J.	101	G	Sept	8
8322 Myers, A.	148	I	Sept	8
8469 Magill, H.	103	I	Sept	10
8596 Morrison, J.	146	E	Sept	12
8627 McKinney, D.	*90*	*C*	*Sept*	*13*
8691 Moritze, A.	146	D	Sept	14
8802 McCollough, —	101	E	Sept	15
9071 Maynard, A.	Art3		Sept	17
9090 McCall, William	Cav22	B	Sept	18
9228 McCullough, S.	138	K	Sept	19
9270 Mayhan, F.	Cav20		Sept	19
9315 Marsh, W.	149	K	Sept	20
9339 Myers, J.A.	138	C	Sept	20
9526 McQuigley, John	101	C	Sept	22
9583 Mead, H.J.	184	B	Sept	23
9598 Martin, J.	Cav17	C	Sept	23
9644 Morris, J.	54	I	Sept	24
9646 Morgan, J.E.	2	A	Sept	24

9651	McCook, B.	118	A	Sept	24	11658 Menk, W.	Cav12	F	Oct	30
9761	McMurray, Wm.	Cav1	I	Sept	25	11683 Morrow, J.C.	Sergnt Major		
9871	Mason, John	112	A	Sept	27		101	E	Oct	31
4578	McKerner, S.	73	A	Aug	2	11684 McCann, J.	Cav11	L	Oct	31
10050	*Mesin, James*	*90*	*F*	*Sept*	*30*	11686 Moore, W.	184	B	Oct	31
10060	Morgan, C.	45	A	Sept	30	11692 Mulligan, J.	7	H	Oct	31
10119	McClany, J.	101	C	Oct	1	11909 McCune, J.	67	E	Nov	8
10154	McElroy, Wm.	Cav13	L	Oct	1	11913 McClush, N.	97	E	Nov	8
10306	Meese, J.	48	A	Oct	4	11982 Manee, M.	53	H	Nov	13
10396	McGraw, John	Art3	A	Oct	6	12008 McCray, J.	145	A	Nov	14
10407	Miller, H	79	K	Oct	6	12088 Maher, D.	118	E	Nov	18
10486	Miller, W.	Cav18	C	Oct	7	12103 Miller, W.	32	I	Nov	22
10610	McKearney, J.W.	118	K	Oct	10	12248 Murray, W.	Cav14	H	Dec	8
10620	McClief, William	7	A	Oct	10	12326 McIntire, J.	55	C	Dec	24
10641	Marker, W.H.	118	D	Oct	10	12334 Myers, A.D.	52	A	Dec	26
10678	Martin, J.P.	7	I	Oct	11	12554 Matthews, J.	Cav6	F	Jan30/65
10684	Miller, James	7	I	Oct	11	12595 Maloy, J.M.	184	D	Feb	5
10803	Mattis, Aaron	138		Oct	12	12625 McGenger, J.	20	C	Feb	9
10825	Moore, C.H.	Cav13	C	Oct	13	12606 Myers, H.	87	E	Feb	23
10929	Martin, George	H.108	I	Oct	14	12771 McDonald, —	9	G	Mar	13
10981	Maxwell, S.	Cav14	B	Oct	15	12806 McGarrett, R.W.	103	F	Feb	21
10991	Moses, W.	Cav16	H	Oct	16	1134 Nicholson, John	Cav3	H	May 16/64
10993	McKnight, James	118	K	Oct	16	1298 Nelson, William	76	H	May	23
11081	Mitchell, J.O.	55	H	Oct	18	2832 Nolti, Wm.	6	F	July	3
11142	Mansfield, George	101	I	Oct	19	3653 Newell, G.S.	183	A	July	20
11229	McClay, J.H,	Cav11	D	Oct	20	4246 Nicholson, W.	Cav1	H	July	29
11305	McBride, —	Cav2	H	Oct	22	4489 Nelson, George	2	K	Aug	1
11326	Marshall, L.	184	A	Oct	23	4936 Naylor, G.W.	Cav13	L	Aug	7
11387	Moore, S.	101	F	Oct	24	5109 Nichols, D.A.	125	D	Aug	9
11459	Moore, J.	Cav13	B	Oct	25	*6001 Neal, H.G.*	*90*	*B*	*Aug*	*17*
11464	McNeise, J.H.	100	E	Oct	26	6011 Nickle, C.	37	G	Aug	17
11542	Miller, F.	54	K	Oct	27	6702 Nickem, James	77	G	Aug	24
11655	Midz, J.	Cav20	A	Oct	30	8154 Naylor, S.	Cav20	H	Sept	8

8907	Noble, J.	73	D	Sept	16	500	Petrisky, H.	54 F	Apr	12
9424	Nice, Isaac	11	L	Sept	21	1110	Patterson, T.	Cav3 A	May	15
9468	Neff, J.	Cav4	D	Sept	21	1119	Patent, Thomas	73 G	May	15
10146	Nelson, G.	55	A	Oct	1	1258	Powell, Wm.	Cav14 D	May	21
10286	Nelson, J.A.	145	G	Oct	4	1556	Powers, John	26 I	June	2
10764	Newberry, John	Cav20	A	Oct	12	1789	Preso, Thomas	26 E	June	9
11107	Nelson, A.	160	E	Oct	18	1884	Powell, Frank	18 E	June	12
11254	Noble, Thomas	Cav19	G	Oct	21	2566	Page, J.	183 G	June	27
11776	Nichols, G.	20	C	Nov	3	2590	Porter, David	101 H	June	28
414	Osbourne, S.K.	4	K	Apr7/64		2903	Parsons, J.T.	103 D	July	5
622	Oglesby, J.	Cav4	K	Apr	19	3197	Painter, J.G.	26 F	July	11
1318	O'Brien, P.	13	A	May	23	3445	Painter, S.	63 A	July	17
1409	Ottinger, I	Cav8	I	May	27	4049	Patterson, R	101 H	July	27
1817	O'Neil, John	69		June	12	4157	Pickett, J.C.	Cav3 A	July	28
2589	Oswald, Stephen	55	G	June	28	4177	Pratt, F.	Cav14 I	July	28
3161	O'Conor, —	83		July	11	4191	Plymeer, W.	Cav20 B	July	28
3199	O'Neil, J.	63	I	July	12	4415	Page, John	112 A	July	31
3704	Olmar, H.	Cav2	H	July	21	4473	Powell, H.	102 H	Aug	1
3861	O'Connor, H.	49	E	July	24	5323	Prosser, J.	63	Aug	11
4161	Owens, G.H.	7	A	July	28	5579	Pyers, Isaac	72 G	Aug	14
5119	*Offlebach, Z.*	*90*	*K*	*Aug*	*9*	5610	Phillips, Jas.	B.101 I	Aug	14
5184	Oliver, W.	103	D	Aug	9	5947	Parish, J.A.	184	Aug	17
5939	O'Hara, M.	101	E	Aug	17	6341	Preans, H.	149 K	Aug	21
6254	O'Connell, Wm.	183	G	Aug	20	6439	Palmer, H.	140 D	Aug	22
6535	O'Hara, John	150	E	Aug	23	6527	Poole, G.	52 B	Aug	22
6658	Oiler, Samuel	103	G	Aug	24	6536	Pifer, M.	13 G	Aug	23
6908	O'Rourke, Chas	109	C	Aug	26	6574	Phillips, J.W.	Cav1 F	Aug	23
7105	Otto, John	Cav5	B	Aug	28	6843	Petersen, G.	103 D	Aug	23
9330	Owens, E.	50	D	Aug	30	6844	Penn, John	Cav5 E	Aug	25
10805	Osborn, E.	Cav11	A	Oct	13	6885	Patten, H.W.	Art2 F	Aug	26
30	Peck, Albert	57	K	Mar 9/64		7118	Potts, Edward	183 H	Aug	28
62	Patterson, Robt	Res2	E	Mar	18	7232	Perkins, N.	103 D	Aug	29
125	Parker, James M.	76	B	Mar	23	8030	Powell, A.T.	149 C	Sept	6

79

8160	Pricht, F.		87	H	Sept 8	1152	Randall, H.	Cav4	H	May 16
8763	Peck, C.W.		145	H	Sept 14	1218	Rigney, Charles	Cav4	G	May 19
8877	Persill, Fred		101		Sept 15	1454	Raleigh, A.	51	G	May 29
9220	Palmer, A.		143	D	Sept 19	1485	Rudolph, S.	Cav13	K	May 30
9684	Perego, W.		143	G	Sept 24	1599	Rhine, George	63	I	June 4
9754	Phipps, J.H.		57	E	Sept 26	1624	Rosenburg, H.	Cav13	H	June 4
10074	Price, G.		106	H	Sept 30	1719	Raymond, John	Cav18	H	June 8
10573	Penstock, A.		144	B	Oct 9	1803	Rheems, A.	73	I	June 10
10858	Powell, I.		101	I	Oct 13	1833	Ramsey, J.D.	103	F	June 11
11168	Price, O.		109	C	Oct 19	1922	Rush, S.	18	G	June 14
11261	Phay, M.		69	C	Oct 21	1942	Robinson, Wm.	77	D	June 14
11637	Phillips, F.		61	K	Oct 28	2225	Roush, Peter	101	E	June 20
11737	Pees, M.T.		145	H	Nov 2	2528	Rupert, F.	Cav2	H	June 26
11833	Penn, J.	Cav18		I	Nov 6	2602	Roat, J.	54	F	June 28
11918	Phelps, W.	Cav4		G	Nov 8	2735	Rhoades, F.	79	E	July 1
11328	Porterfield, J.	Cav5		M	Oct 23	2911	Rock, J.E.	5	M	July 5
12075	Pencer, W.		18	C	Nov 18	2979	Rogart, John	Cav13	E	July 7
12191	Pryor, Wm.		11	C	Nov 28	3103	Ray, A.	77	E	July 17
12359	Poleman, H.	Cav1		F	Dec 30	3024	Rugh, M.J.	103	D	July 7
12378	Perry, H.		121	C	Jan2/65	3270	Robins, R.	69	B	July 13
12388	Pritchett, J.		72	C	Jan 8	3468	Ransom, H.	148	I	July 17
12479	Potter, B.F.		148	I	Jan	3827	Rinner, L.	Cav5	A	July 23
6756	Quinby, L.C.		76	E	Aug 64	4074	Ringwalk, J.F.	79	H	July 27
47	Reed, Sam	Cav4		D	Mar 10	4241	Roger, L.	115	L	July 29
126	Robertson, J.		119	K	Mar 23	4309	Rogers, C.	73	C	July 30
132	Ros4enburg, Henry		49	G	Mar 24	4476	Ray, James R.	184	B	Aug 1
171	Reign, John		83	K	Mar 26	4507	Riese, S.	103	D	Aug 1
308	Richpeder, A.		13	B	Apr 2	4844	Richie, James	103	B	Aug 6
610	Ray, William	Cav8		F	Apr 18	4940	Ruthfer, J.	Art2	F	Aug 7
847	Rhinehart, J.		3	D	May 3	5319	Rice, Samuel	101	K	Aug 11
895	Russell, F.		4	D	May 3	5389	Ross, David	103	B	Aug 12
907	Rhinehgolt, J.	Cav18		I	May 5	5430	Robinson, John	99	D	Aug 12
940	Robinson, C.W.		150	E	May 7	5537	Rose, B.	13	I	Aug 13

80

5800	Robins, J.	Cav2	M	Aug	15
5879	Rider, H.	Cav7	L	Aug	16
5894	Richards, E.	143	E	Aug	16
5912	Reese, Jacob	103	B	Aug	17
5940	Richards, John	Cav1	G	Aug	17
6321	Robbins, G.	106	G	Aug	21
6373	Roger, John L.	110	H	Aug	21
6520	Reynolds, J.	14	H	Aug	22
6725	Rowe, E.	103	A	Aug	24
6777	Rangardener, J.	149	H	Aug	25
6789	Richards, G.	Cav13	A	Aug	25
6790	Runels, John	Cav6	L	Aug	25
6822	Rum, A.	188	C	Aug	25
6838	Reese, D	148	K	Aug	25
6896	Raiff, T.	1	A	Aug	26
6933	Richardson, —	61		Aug	26
7067	Reese, D.	143	F	Aug	28
7202	Ruff, J.	103	F	Aug	29
7292	Redmire, H.	98	B	Aug	30
7293	Robins, George	62	A	Aug	30
7410	Richardson, H.	103	K	Aug	31
7467	Richard, D.	Cav18	D	Sept	1
7716	Rice, E.	7	B	Sept	3
7738	Roads, Fred.	101	E	Sept	3
8139	Rathburn, K.	2	F	Sept	8
8540	Russell, S.A.	79	A	Sept	12
8545	Ray, A.	149	D	Sept	12
8602	Richards, J.	106	H	Sept	12
8635	Rhangmen, G.	138	D	Sept	13
8742	Root, D.	48	B	Sept	14
9019	Ret, George	18	A	Sept	17
9272	Ramsay, J.I.	149		Sept	19
9585	Richie, H.	11	F	Sept	23

9599	Renamer, W.E.	87	H	Sept	23
9612	Richards, John	113	D	Sept	23
9653	Reed, R.	103	A	Sept	24
9766	Ramsay, R.	84	D	Sept	25
9882	Richards, J.	53	K	Sept	27
10174	Reed, J.	55	A	Oct	1
10863	Ramsay, Wm.	87	B	Oct	13
10622	Reedy, E.T.	87	B	Oct	10
10935	Roundabush, H.B.	51	A	Oct	14
10947	Rockwell, A.	Cav2	L	Oct	14
11071	Raeff, J.B.	72	E	Oct	17
11115	Rincle, John A.	20	A	Oct	18
11293	Rolston, J.	18	F	Oct	22
11147	Rudy, J.	13	F	Oct	19
11444	Rifle, S.G.	189	C	Oct	25
11566	Richardson, A	144	E	Oct	27
11868	Rowland, N.	111	F	Nov	6
12008	Rapp, A.E.	Cav18	I	Nov	15
12048	Ruth, B.S.	23	I	Nov	16
12206	Rothe, C.	101	A	Dec	1
12355	Reese, D.	7	A	Dec	29
12372	Reed, W.S.	128	H	Jan1/65
377	Smith, M.D.	18	B	Apr5/64
788	Smith, George	Cav5	H	Apr	28
881	Smith, William	4	A	May	4
882	Smith, T.	19	G	May	4
921	Steffler, W.J.	Cav12	G	May	6
1014	Serend, H	Cav4	D	May	10
1030	Shebert, Gottlieb	73	C	May	11
1058	Spilyfiter, A.	54	F	May	13
1105	Sullivan, D.	101	K	May	15
1114	Shindle, S.R.	140	K	May	15
1155	Stearner, E.K.	Cav14	A	May	16

1169	Sloat, B.		76	I	May	16	3113	Sweet, H.	57 K July 10
1175	Scott, William		4	B	May	16	3136	Shoemaker, M.	148 G July 10

1169 Sloat, B.   76 I May 16   3113 Sweet, H.   57 K July 10

Number	Name	Unit	Co.	Date		Number	Name	Reg./Unit	Co. Date
1169	Sloat, B.	76	I	May 16		3113	Sweet, H.	57	K July 10
1175	Scott, William	4	B	May 16		3136	Shoemaker, M.	148	G July 10
1216	Severn, C.	139	A	May 19		3154	Sillers, Wm.	77	D July 11
1256	Sammoris, B.	Cav2	B	May 21		3214	Stone, W.F.	53	G July 12
1349	Smith, Charles	26	A	May 24		3480	Swelser, J.	103	D July 17
1453	Schlenbough, C.	Cav4	G	May 29		3567	Smalley, L.	58	K July 19
1503	Smith, Martin	Cav18	H	May 31		3568	Stevens, S.G.	150	H July 19
1535	Stone, Samuel	26	F	June 1		3586	Sickles, Daniel	116	K July 19
1543	Shoemaker, M.	Cav13	H	June 1		3632	Serders, J.S.	142	K July 20
1605	Swearer, G.	13	H	June 4		3670	Stopper, Wm.	16	B July 20
1620	Schiefeit, Jacob	54	F	June 4		3763	Stillenberger, F.	172	F July 22
1632	Schmar, R.	45	F	June 5		3775	Strance, D.	11	H July 22
1963	Smith, D	Cav11	H	June 14		3855	Smith, J.	79	F July 24
2039	Slough, H.	53		June 15		3906	Smith, O.C.	77	G July 24
2070	Stevens, A.	Cav13	M	June 16		3956	Seilk, A.	144	D July 25
2121	Sherwood, C.H.	Cav4	M	June 17		3960	Sullivan, T.	77	F July 25
2123	Stall, Samuel	75	D	June 17		4006	Smith, F.	64	K July 26
2126	Say, J.R.	Cav4	K	June 17		4009	Shafer, J.H.	84	E July 26
2163	Steele, J.S.	Cav7	F	June 19		4012	Shapely, George	103	G July 26
2259	Scoles, M.	27	K	June 21		4043	Strickley, C.	53	J July 27
2331	Sims, B.	Cav14	G	June 22		4064	Shriveley, E.S.	Cav19	M July 27
2412	Shop, Jacob	2	M	June 24		4113	Sheppard, E.	145	G July 28
2622	Springer, John	101	E	June 28		4164	Smith, S.W.	101	B July 28
2650	Stewart, J.B.	103	A	June 29		4213	Shaffer, Peter	52	F July 29
2725	Scott, Allen	150	H	July 1		4223	Shister, F.	Cav3	A July 29
2738	Schimgert, J.	73	G	July 1		4228	Stein, J.	7	G July 29
2791	Shimer, J.A.	Cav13	A	July 2		4274	Sloan, J.	11	E July 29
2864	Scott, Wm. Negro	8	D	July 4		4285	Shone, P.	Cav4	D July 30
2905	Stump, A.	11	I	July 5		4345	Stobbs, W.W.	101	E July 30
2941	Smith, Jacob	51	H	July 6		4348	Scott, A.	22	F July 31
2982	Shaw, W.	140	B	July 7		4351	Scundler, J.	67	A July 31
2999	Smulley, John	112	K	July 7		4372	Smith, P.	72	C July 31
3057	Sutton, R.M.	103	I	July 9		4566	Sale, Thomas	15	M Aug 2

4775	Shink, James	81	F	Aug	5	6823	Spain, Richard	118 H Aug	25
4791	Sullivan, Ed	67	H	Aug	5	6829	Sturgess, W.A.	79 G Aug	25
4797	Scar, C.	Cav14	L	Aug	5	6880	Stuler, D.	Cav4 A Aug	26
4845	Shember, John	Cav11	D	Aug	6	7029	Strickler, J.W.	11 F Aug	27
4928	Slicker, J.	77	D	Aug	6	7106	Smith, John F.	55 C Aug	28
4931	Sheit, P	61	G	Aug	7	7137	Sloan, J.M.	Cav18 D Aug	28
4945	Swartz, P.	27	I	Aug	7	7141	Springer, J.	113 F Aug	29
5160	Stiner, John	Cav22	G	Aug	9	7262	Shriver, B.	Cav18 K Aug	30
5189	Striker, F.	Cav14	A	Aug	9	7302	Singer, J.	Art2 A Aug	30
5215	Sworeland, Wm.	184	A	Aug	10	7358	Scoleton, J.	53 F Aug	31
5232	Speck, A.	118	A	Aug	10	7363	Sweeney, D.	Cav14 E Aug	31
5411	Shaffer,Daniel	Cav13	F	Aug	12	7379	Scott, W.B.	Cav4 D Aug	31
5529	Spangrost, A.	103	D	Aug	12	7631	Streetman, J.	7 E Sept	2
5437	Shears, J.S.	149	K	Aug	12	7638	Steele, J.	62 M Sept	2
5463	Stibbs, W.	56	H	Aug	13	7648	Spencer, George	20 C Sept	3
5494	Shape, F.	Cav18	A	Aug	13	7662	Snyder, M.S.	183 A Sept	3
5603	Somerfield, W.	69	E	Aug	14	7705	Swartz, George	Cav5 A Sept	3
5700	Stinebach, A.	150	C	Aug	15	7770	Stockhouse, D.	Cav18 I Sept	4
5750	Spears, W.M.	Cav2	K	Aug	15	7905	Sellers, H.	149 G Sept	5
5874	Sheppard, N.	79	F	Aug	16	7939	Shultz, John	Cav4 I Sept	5
5965	Shultz, F.	Cav13	K	Aug	17	7960	Smith, A.C.	7 F Sept	6
6205	Shoop, G.	103	K	Aug	19	8038	Simpson, T.	53 K Sept	6
6289	Smith, H.	26	K	Aug	20	8103	Stump, J.	105 I Sept	7
6337	Smith, W.	Cav18	B	Aug	21	8112	Slade, E.	150 H Sept	7
6382	Swager, M.	101	F	Aug	21	8444	Shirk, M.B.	142 A Sept	11
6436	Spain, Thomas	118	H	Aug	22	8567	Simons, Wm. H.	76 K Sept	12
6523	Stover, J.	49	F	Aug	22	8659	*Spould, E.*	*90 E Sept 13*
6526	Stahler, S.	149	G	Aug	22	8773	Smith, Wm.	2 K Sept	14
6534	Snyder, John	118	C	Aug	23	8795	Stella, J.F.	1 B Sept	15
6584	Sloate, E.	50	D	Aug	23	9296	Signall, —	79 H Sept	19
6595	Shirley, Henry	105	I	Aug	23	9012	Steadman, W.	54 F Sept	17
6669	Sherwood, P.	84	I	Aug	24	9123	Schably, J.	54 A Sept	18
6776	Shellito, R.	150	C	Aug	25	9138	Shoup, S.	Cav16 B Sept	18

9310	Smith, Charles	7	H	Sept	20	11792	Sellentine, M.	145	C	Nov 4
9365	Stebbins, Z.	7	H	Sept	20	11825	Seltzer, D.	20	K	Nov 5
9411	Scott, D.	149	G	Sept	21	11885	Smith, W.B.	Cav14	E	Nov 6
9567	Snyder, A.	148	I	Sept	23	11890	Shure, J.P.	184	F	Nov 7
9593	Sternholt, Wm.	38		Sept	23	11895	Snively, G.W.	Cav20	F	Nov 7
9742	Supple, C.M.	63	B	Sept	25	11926	Scover, J.H.	79	G	Nov 8
9780	Surplus, W.	Cav13	L	Sept	26	11951	Shefiley, W.	118	G	Nov 9
9890	Siherk, Christian	145		Sept	27	12057	Stitzer, G.	2	E	Nov 16
9898	Sweeny, W.P.	Cav13		Sept	27	12081	Stensley, D.	184	A	Nov 18
9912	Sanford, C.	69	H	Sept	28	12217	Smith, J.S.	118	F	Dec 3
9985	Sheppard, C.	118	E	Sept	29	12218	Skinner, S.O.	77	A	Dec 4
10088	Sloan, P.	115	A	Sept	30	12282	Shafer, T.	184	E	Dec 13
10132	Smith, J.S.	Cav22	B	Oct	1	12308	Stafford, W.	67	H	Dec 19
10299	Strong, H.	55	E	Oct	4	12384	Sourbeer, J.E.	20	A	Jan3/65
10323	Smith, E.	10	H	Oct	4	12590	Sipe, F.	87	C	Feb 5
10516	Snyder, Wm.	54	H	Oct	8	12598	Stauffer, J.	1	K	Feb 6
10525	Stones, T.	121	K	Oct	8	12648	Stain, G.W.	Cav20	K	Feb 13
10530	Smallwood, C.	7	F	Oct	8	12669	Slough, E.B.	Cav1	D	Feb 17
10609	Small, H.	101	H	Oct	10	12670	Scott, A.J.	14	D	Feb 17
10720	Smallman, J.W.	63	A	Oct	11	12676	Sheridan, M.	103	F	Feb 19
10808	Steele, F.F.	Cav20	A	Oct	12	12817	Sharks, J.N.	14	D	Mar 27
10837	Shank, A.	184	C	Oct	13	12824	Shultz, H.H.	87	A	Apr 5/65
11044	Smith, Andrew	Cav22	B	Oct	17	778	Thistlewood, J.	73	E	Apr28/64
11069	Stevens, C.P.	11	A	Oct	17	785	Tolland, D	Cav13	D	Apr 28
11233	SAmith, H.W.	53	B	Oct	21	1144	Taylor, J.F.	13	E	May 16
11246	Smith, James	57	E	Oct	21	1145	Tull, D.	4	D	May 16
11355	Silvy, David	Cav18	I	Oct	23	1153	Toner, Peter	10	A	May 16
11368	Seyoff, H.	81	C	Oct	23	1814	Thompson, H.	57	C	June 10
11488	Sunderland, E.	11	D	Oct	26	2182	Thompson, A. Mus.	Cav4	C	June 19
11529	Stevenson, John	111	I	Oct	26	2302	Townsend, D.	Cav18	D	June 22
11661	Speck, Olive	67	H	Oct	30	2635	Tyser, L.	145	D	June 29
11741	Smith, H.	183	D	Nov	2	2897	Terwilliger, E	103	H	July 5
11785	Snodgrass, R.J.	145	H	Nov	4	3003	Thompson, R.	103	F	July 7

47	Taylor, C.W.	84	D	May	24
3329	Titus, W.	171	D	July	14
3473	Todd, Wm.	103	K	July	17
3571	Thompson, J.S.	183	H	July	19
3768	Terrell, A.	Cav12	B	July	22
3968	Trumbull, H.	3	E	July	25
4116	Thompson,James	Cav18	G	July	28
4160	Tinsdale, —	149	E	July	28
4713	Thompson, J.	Art3	A	Aug	4
5179	Thompson, W.W.	101	B	Aug	9
5345	Thomas, F.	7	F	Aug	11
5966	Thompson, J.B.	100	H	Aug	17
6146	Thompson, F.A.B.	69	I	Aug	19
6447	Tubbs, E.	143	I	Aug	23
6476	Toll, William	Res11	I	Aug	22
6791	Turner, John	118	H	Aug	25
7250	Thomas, E.	23	F	Aug	30
7400	Thorpe, L.	61	E	Aug	31
7904	Trash, Seth	81	A	Sept	6
8231	Truman, E.W.	9	G	Sept	9
8531	Tilt, W.	115	A	Sept	12
8619	Tutor, C.	184	A	Sept	13
9027	Tits, P.		C	Sept	17
9212	Thorpe, D.	18	D	Sept	19
9302	Thompson, H.	Cav18	I	Sept	20
9726	Tonson, J.	99	B	Sept	25
9775	Thuck, I.	7	C	Sept	26
9981	Tones, E.	145	F	Sept	26
10008	*Thompson, J.*	*90*	*H*	*Sept*	*29*
10725	Tibbels, George	69	K	Oct	11
11002	Thatcher, R.	14	C	Oct	16
11407	Thompson, J.	Cav12	E	Oct	24
11754	Trespan, P.	67	H	Nov	2

12080	Townsend, C	103	F	Nov	18
971	Ulrick, John	17	E	May	9
4184	Urndraugh, W.	4	H	July	28
12133	Utter, William		H	Nov	23
1369	Ventler, Charles		G	May	25
7739	Vogel, L		A	June	8
2428	Vernon, S.	7	K	June	24
4245	Vanholt, T.	13	A	July	29
5392	Vandeby, B.	7	A	Aug	12
6877	Vanderpool, F.	57	B	Aug	26
8270	Vail, G.B.	77	G	Sept	9
8791	Vaughan, J.	108	F	Sept	15
8948	Varndale, J.	112	A	Sept	16
9688	Vandier, Wm.	Phila.		Sept	24
57	Wilkins, A.	Cav12	L	Mar	17
128	Waterman, John	88	B	Mar	23
193	Wise, Isaac	18	G	Mar	27
496	Wheeler, J	110	I	Apr	12
516	Warren, J.	76	A	Apr	12
587	Weed, A.B.	4	K	Apr	17
657	Wentworth, James	83	G	Apr	21
665	Watson, F.F.	2	B	Apr	22
686	Wahl, John	73	C	Apr	23
764	Wilson, John	Cav14	H	Apr	27
852	Williams, S.	Cav18	I	May	3
941	Wolf, J.H.	Cav13	H	May	7
1021	Wright, J.	Cav12	B	May	11
1067	Whitton, Robt.	145	C	May	13
1093	Wright, Wm.	Cav16	A	May	14
1386	Wymans, James	150	C	May	26
1387	Wilson, James	Cav13	D	May	26
1443	Williams, F.	Cav3	B	May	28
1494	Williams, Fred.	101	K	May	30

No.	Name	Regiment	Co.	Date
1525	Wallace, H.	Cav13	H	May 31
1563	Waltermeyer, H.	76	H	June 2
1721	Whitney, W.	83	A	June 8
1749	Woodsides, W.I.	18	E	June 9
1791	Wolf, Samuel	77	A	June 10
1903	Woodward, G.W.	Cav3		June 13
1977	Wyant, H.	103	G	June 15
2338	Walters, C.	73	B	June 22
2616	Williams, J.	83	F	June 28
2699	Whitaker, —Negro	8		July 2
2937	Whitaker, S.	96	E	July 6
3023	Weider, L.	50	H	July 7
3135	Wallace, A.	116	I	July 10
3277	Wright, W.A.	Cav20	G	July 14
3384	Woodruff, W.D.	103	B	July 16
3392	Wait, George	Cav1	G	July 16
3605	Walker, E.	7	A	July 19
3694	White, E.D.	Cav2	H	July 21
4181	Wisel, M.	Cav18	K	July 28
4338	Ward, Daniel	138	E	July 30
3880	White, M.	7	C	July 24
3822	Wilson, Andrew	103	H	July 23
4069	Wolf, A.	146	D	July 27
4046	Winegardner, A.	73	G	July 27
3921	Wilson, Wm.	43		July 25
4428	Williams, George	54	H	July 31
4702	Wilebrough, E.	148	I	Aug 4
4828	Ward, P.	103	B	Aug 6
4966	Wetherholt, C.	54	F	Aug 7
4981	Waserun, G.	Cav4	I	Aug 7
4996	White, S.	Cav14	B	Aug 7
5106	*Weaver, James*	*90*	*K*	*Aug 9*
5353	Wilks, S.	77	G	Aug 11
5458	Wilson, William	7	K	Aug 12
5677	Weeks, D.	53	G	Aug 14
6050	Williams, —	7	A	Aug 18
6052	Waterhouse, W.	Cav3	L	Aug 18
6133	Workman, A.	118	D	Aug 19
6305	Whipple, H.	18	B	Aug 20
6427	Wart, C.	143	E	Aug 22
6530	Winerman, James	77	A	Aug 23
6563	Wible, Paul	57	A	Aug 23
6626	Walker, S.A.	103	I	Aug 23
6808	Wick, R.C.	103	E	Aug 25
6980	Woolslaer, W.H.	77	C	Aug 27
6981	White, James P.	149	D	Aug 27
7023	Woodford, J.A.	101	E	Aug 27
7277	White, Ed	103	K	Aug 30
7382	Webb, J.S.	69	K	Aug 31
7386	Walton, A. (Ser)	Cav4	A	Aug 31
7680	Wallwork, T.	118	D	Sept 3
7714	Warner, L.	Cav5	C	Sept 5
7799	Wynn, H.	101	F	Sept 5
7809	Wiggins, D.	Art2	D	Sept 5
7914	Weekland, F.	101	K	Sept 5
7933	Wade, George W.	118	E	Sept 5
8081	Weber, W.	116	F	Sept 7
8360	White, D.	Art2	D	Sept 10
8879	Wheeler, J.	7	C	Sept 15
9091	Wheeler, C.C.	Cav14	M	Sept 18
9343	Williams, W.	20		Sept 20
9434	Wilson, W.H.	3	I	Sept 21
9534	Woolman, H.	Cav18	A	Sept 23
9573	Wingert, C.	111	I	Sept 23
9634	Wismer, J.	100	A	Sept 24
9657	Wilson, G.M.	Cav7	M	Sept 24

9825 Walke, G.	Cav4 K Sept 27	12129 Webb, C.H. (Ser)	101 H Nov 23
9909 Wentley, J.	155 G Sept 28	12222 Williams, J.	145 A Dec 4
10022 Watson, William	99 I Sept 30	12137 Wood, J.M.	2 A Nov 23
10227 Weeks, C.	76 F Oct 2	12380 Watson, H.	184 A Jan2/65
10229 Waltzs, J.	7 H Oct 2	12485 Williams, B.	75 B Jan 19
10236 Weekly, John	14 A Oct 2	12493 Walker, N.C.	87 B Jan 20
10315 Wolfhope, J.	184 A Oct 3	10158 Van Dyke, D.L.	103 A Oct 1/64
10400 Wilson, G.	55 C Oct 6	11810 Vanmarkes, D	6 E Nov 4
10426 Wilson, J.	118 D Oct 6	12154 Vanhatterman, I.	4 G Nov 25
10521 Williams, W.	46 K Oct 8	3958 Vogle, V.	78 D July 25
10568 Walk, W.	87 E Oct 9	3799 Yocumbs, W.B.	93 B July 22
10632 Welsy, John M.	116 E Oct 10	4900 Yocum, D.	Cav1 M Aug 6
10659 Watts, A.J.	Cav12 I Oct 11	6103 Yingling, E.	78 E Aug 18
10729 White, J.M.	21 G Oct 11	6546 Yeager, Samuel	158 D Aug 23
10797 Walker, Wm.	148 B Oct 12	10204 Young, J.B.	49 G Oct 2
9464 Warner, Cyrus W.	184 B Oct 21	11040 Young, W.H.	145 F Oct 17
10840 Wright, Wm.	16 I Oct 13	11872 Yeager, J.	49 C Nov 6
10902 Wolford, D.	54 K Oct 14	1806 Zerphy, J.	79 E June 10
10974 Watson, C.	184 E Oct 15	4255 Zimmerman, B.	148 B July 23
11048 Wilderman, E.	14 D Oct 17	6573 Zane, William	19 K Aug 23
11108 Walker, A.	45 D Oct 18	4818 Zeri, S.	103 F Aug 25
11129 Wilson, G.	140 F Oct 18	11327 Zane, M.	118 E Oct 23
11498 Warrington, J.H.	106 H Oct 26		
11503 Waiter, W.	184 F Oct 26		
11557 Wood, J. (Ser)	19 C Oct 27		
11722 Woodburn, D.J.	7 G Nov 1		
11750 Wyncoop, F.P.	7 I Nov 2		
11899 Webster, J.(Ser)	Cav20 L Nov 2		
11978 Wilkinson, C.(Ser)	104 I Nov 7		
11987 Weaver, J.	53 K Nov 13		
12095 Walder, John	Cav5 L Nov 19		
12098 Wider, N.H.	184 F Nov 19		
12123 Weatherald, H.W.	7 F Nov 22		

The Blue And The Gray

By Francis M. Finch

By the flow of the inland river,
Whence the fleets of iron have
fled,
Where the blades of the grave–grass
quiver,
Asleep are the ranks of the dead.
Under the sod and the dew,
Waiting the judgment day—
Under the one, the blue;
Under the other, the gray.

These in the robings of glory,
Those in the gloom of defeat,
All with the battle–blood gory,
In the dusk of eternity meet.
Under the sod and the dew,
Waiting the judgment day—
Under the laurel, the blue;
Under the willow the gray.

From the silence of sorrowful
hours
The desolate mourners go,
Lovingly laden with flowers,
Alike for the friend and foe.
Under the sod and the dew,
Waiting the judgment day—
Under the roses, the blue;
Under the lilies, the gray.

So with an equal splendor,
The morning sun rays fall,
With a touch impartially tender,
On the blossoms blooming for all.
Under the sod and dew,
Waiting the judgment day—
Broidered with gold the blue;
Mellowed with gold, the gray.

So when summer calleth
On forest and field of grain,
With an equal
murmur falleth,
The cooling drip of rain.
Under the sod and the dew,
Waiting the judgment day—
Wet with the rain, the blue;
Wet with the rain, the gray.

Sadly, but not with upbraiding,
The generous deed was done;
In the storm of the years that
are fading,
No braver battle was won.
Under the sod and the dew,
Waiting the judgment day—
Under the blossoms, the blue;
Under the garlands, the gray.

No more shall the war-cry sever,
Or the winding rivers be red;
They banish our anger forever
When they laurel the graves of
our dead.
Under the sod and the dew,
Waiting the judgment day—
Love and tears for the blue;
Tears and love for the gray!